THE TURNING THANKS COOKBOOK

two peas
publishing

ISBN: 978-0-9837610-6-8

Cover and Interior design © 2011 Paula Rozelle Hanback

Neither Mt. Wesley Akin Nazarene Church nor Two Peas Publishing have any copyright interest of any nature or kind whatsoever in the cookbook, the recipes, or other printed material provided to us.

Copyright of individual recipes or other material contained in this book remain the property of the person or persons who submitted the material.

Neither Mt. Wesley Akin Nazarene Church nor Two Peas Publishing make any warranty or representation of any nature or kind whatsoever relating to the recipes, the ingredients in each recipe, the directions and/or instructions for preparing each recipe and disclaims and excludes any and all implied warranties of the results of the use of each recipe or of the fitness of the product produced by utilization of any recipe for a particular purpose. Neither Mt. Wesley Akin Nazarene Church nor Two Peas Publishing warrant that the recipes or any one of them will meet users' requirements or expectations or that the recipes are without defect or error.

DEDICATION

To all members of the Mt. Wesley Akin family
Past, Present, and Future

FOREWORD

When families from the American South gather around the dinner table, the meal is often preceded by a short lull in conversation that is soon broken by the following interrogatory prompt: "who wants to turn thanks?" Just as often, the prompt might be directed at someone in particular, such as "Jim, will you turn thanks?"

What we actually mean when we utter those words is: "will someone please step up and take the lead in thanking our Lord for the food that we are about to consume?" Essentially, we are returning gratitude for the bountiful harvest before us. We are "turning thanks."

Praying done, it is then time to eat. The silence and solemnity that preceded the meal is replaced by the clatter of forks, spoons, and knives against pots, pans, and dishes; not to mention the thrum of conversation and hearty laughter that always accompanies the gatherings of loved ones.

You won't find much on the Internet about "turning thanks" as a colloquialism. A general Google search for the phrase results in a single blog post about the phrase itself. The next few hundred results feature sentences that end with the word

"turning" followed by a new sentence that begins with the word "Thanks."

No matter. We know what we mean by it.

Most importantly, the receiver of our gratitude knows what we mean by it.

Situated among the rolling hills of Southern Middle Tennessee, Mt. Wesley Akin Nazarene Church is often home to exactly the kind of gatherings and gratefulness that God inspires. In the pages that follow, you will find a few of the many favorite recipes that the families of the church turn thanks for on a regular basis. And you will learn a little about the church and our community along the way.

So get out your pots, pans, and dishes. Polish up those forks, spoons, and knives. And bring your appetite. There's good eatin' and friendly folks waiting just inside.

Who wants to turn thanks?

—*James R. Hanback, Jr.*

ACKNOWLEDGEMENTS

Many people contribute to the creation of a book such as this — so many that it becomes almost impossible to thank them all without fear of leaving someone out.

Above all else, we thank our Lord and Savior, Jesus Christ. To Him belongs all the glory.

We also wish to thank all the members and friends of Mt. Wesley Akin Nazarene Church, both past and present, for contributing their recipes and stories, information, facts, and photos for this publication.

Special thanks to James Hanback, Sr. and Shirley Hanback for compiling and typing all the recipes. Jimmy also compiled all the historical information and pictures — both enormous tasks.

Thanks to Paula Rozelle Hanback for doing the design and layout, and James Hanback, Jr. for writing the Foreword. James and Paula's publishing company, Two Peas Publishing, provided the publication services at no charge, for which we are very grateful.

Finally, thanks to David and Michelle Usry and to David and Carrie Dhanarajan, for their service to the church and its members.

INTRODUCTION

Over time, documentation and historical information can get lost or forgotten. This book is an effort to not only provide a unique glimpse into the culture of Mt. Wesley Akin Nazarene Church through our recipes, but also an effort to pull together everything we know about this history of the Mt. Wesley and Akin Nazarene Churches, two independent entities that eventually formed the church as it is today.

I became involved with Mt. Wesley Church in 1962, shortly after obtaining my driver license. I was dating a young lady at that time, whom I married in 1965 and who has stuck by me ever since. Her family involvement with the church dated back to its founding. To see her on Sundays and on Wednesday nights, I had to attend church. It was something I was not sure I wanted because I come from a long line of Evangelical (Southern) Baptists. What I had heard about Nazarenes was a little disturbing. The Nazarenes began life as The Pentecostal Church of the Nazarene. Women did not wear makeup and were not allowed to cut their hair. Dancing was not allowed. Neither were movies. Television was also bad thing. What was I getting myself into?

Fortunately, some things had changed by the time I got involved. All things considered, it now seems like sticking around was the right thing for me to do. It is 2011 as I write this and I remain a part of Mt. Wesley Akin Nazarene.

It was still winter that first time I walked into Mt. Wesley back in 1962. It was cold outside. And inside. The church at that time was a one-room building and had not changed much since its construction in 1878. A potbelly stove that stood in the front left corner of the building contained the only source of warmth, a roaring fire that Brother Hubert Haywood, a Church elder, arrived early on Sunday morning to build and stoke. By the time the parishioners arrived, the front of the building was warm, but the back—where all us young folks sat—remained frigid. I could not stop shivering.

Sunday School began at 10 o'clock sharp. Brother Frank Caperton was responsible for that. Everything—Sunday School, service, and the pastor's message—happened in that one room. The morning service started promptly at 11. Brother Haywood led the singing and the Rev. Everett P. Boyett preached the message.

The pews were solid wood and uncomfortable. The songbooks were old and tattered. And it was cold. But a miracle of sorts happened in that little one-room church that day. The

congregation sang the old hymns at the top of their lungs and the preacher launched into an old-time sermon. By the time it was all over, I was no longer cold. At first I attributed my warmth to the church service, but now I believe some of it was the proximity of the young lady sitting beside me.

Much has changed at that little church since 1962. Many of the old records and histories have been lost. The older generations that can remember those days are gradually fading away. All this has prompted me to reconstruct as much information as I possibly can. Lifelong friendships have been ignited and fond memories have been stoked at this old church. I am sure there are many more to come, so please forgive me if the historical narratives in this book sometimes devolve into nostalgia.

The histories of the churches and of religion in general around Santa Fe, Tennessee, are so interwoven between denominations, ministers, families, and friends that it is necessary to include information about others in this writing. One cannot fully understand how a particular church began and developed into what it is today without that information.

Mt. Wesley Akin Nazarene Church began life as The Missionary Methodist, but the same people and places are involved. Trying to find a starting point was overwhelming.

Over time, the buildings have changed, the names of the churches have changed, and the sizes and compositions of the congregations have ebbed and flowed. All the changes blur our memories of the past and of our rich heritage. After a time, it gets difficult to find our roots for the foliage.

Therefore, let me suggest that you try something after you taste a few of our recipes and while you ponder this history and the old photographs contained within these pages. If you get a chance go to the church when it is quiet and empty, sit down in a pew, close your eyes, and relax. Let your mind wander back to those early years. Visualize the old buildings, the old time preachers, the congregations. Listen to the old Gospel singings and sermons. Sing your favorite hymn to yourself or quote your favorite Bible verse.

When you leave, you just might be a changed person.

Families were started and raised in these churches. The echoes of family, friends, and acquaintances are all present in them.

Remember, they passed this way too!

—*James R. Hanback, Sr.*

CONTENTS

Healing Foods of the Bible xxi

Healing Checklist xxxiii

Appetizers and Beverages
Baked Corn Dip 2
Possum Dip 3
Sausage Balls 4
Sausage Cheese Dip 5
Pineapple Cheese Ball 6
Frances' Punch 7
Banana Crush Punch 8
Orange Punch 9
Lemon Punch 10
MaMa's Christmas Punch . . 11
Hot Cranberry Tea 12
Dutch Oven Hot Cider 13
Boiled Custard 14

Breads
"Red Lobster" Biscuits 20
Homemade Biscuits 21
Hawaiian Sweet Rolls 22
Quick Rolls 24
Louise's Spoon Rolls 25
One Hour Rolls 26
Dinner Rolls 27
Corn Cornbread 28
Zucchini Bread 30
Banana Bread 1 31
Banana Bread 2 32
Banana Bread 3 33
Ginger Bread 34
Breakfast Pizza 35

Preserves

Catfish Campus	Aunt Ola's Closet Pickles... 43
Tomato Pickle 40	Pickled Beets 44
Catfish Relish 41	Christmas Jam 45
Corn Relish 42	Pear Honey 46

Soups and Salads

Chili with Tomato........ 52	Marinated Vegetable Salad . 60
Vegetable Beef Stew....... 53	Summer Slaw............ 61
Salvation Soup	Cabbage Salad........... 62
—Vegeterian............. 54	Lemon Cabbage Salad..... 63
Corn Chowder........... 55	Buttermilk Salad 64
Seven Layer Salad 56	Jell-O Salad............. 65
Broccoli Salad 1.......... 57	Orange Salad............ 66
Broccoli Salad 2.......... 58	Pretzel Salad 67
Broccoli and	Fruit Salad.............. 68
Cauliflower Salad 59	Mandarin Almond Salad... 69

Entrees

Poke and Eggs........... 74	Tender Pork Chops
Boiled Country Ham	and Gravy 79
(Lard Stand) 75	Quick Sweet & Sour Pork.. 80
Baked Ham 76	Speedy Stir Fry Beef 81
Oven Baked Country Ham . 77	Rib Eye Roast & Oven
Honey-Pecan Pork Cutlets . 78	Browned Vegetables....... 82

Reece's Slow Cook
Pot Roast 84
Beef Stroganoff 85
Pepper Steak 86
Braised Sirloin Tips
over Rice 87
Jim's Meatloaf 88
Thrifty Meatballs 89
Easy Stuffed Peppers 90
Stuffed Tomatoes 91
Easy Lasagna 92
Baked Hot Chicken Salad . . 93
Chicken Casserole 1 94
Chicken Casserole 2 95
Chicken Casserole 3 96
Chicken Casserole 4 97
Chicken Enchiladas 98
Lemon Garlic Chicken 99
Turkey Divan 100
Garlic Salmon Fillet 101
Baked Cod 102
Meal in One 103
Mexican Meal in One
(Casserole) 104
Farmer's Strata 105
Veggie Pot Pie 106
Island Burger 108
Soupy Burger 109
Hamburber BBQ 110

Sides

Scalloped Oysters 116
Ronald Reagan's Favorite
Mac and Cheese 117
Pasta with Broccoli
and Pine Nuts 118
Wild Rice Medley 119
Cornbread & Sausage
Stuffing 120
Corn Casserole 121
Mixed Vegetable
Casserole 122
Green Bean Casserole 123
Green Beans 124
Cowboy Baked Beans 125
Potato Salad
— Old Fashioned 126
Potato Pancakes 127
BLT Potatoes 128

Parmesan Potatoes....... 129	Stuffed Mushrooms....... 133
Hash Brown Casserole ... 130	Sweet Potato Bake....... 134
Ratatouille............. 131	Sweet Potatoes.......... 135
Squash Casserole........ 132	Sweet Milk Gravy........ 136

Desserts

Carrot Cake 1 142	Peach Cobbler 163
Carrot Cake 2 143	Blueberry Dump Cake ... 164
Coconut Cake 144	Pie Pastry.............. 165
Easy Coconut Cake...... 146	Old-Fashioned Chess Pie . 166
Dark Chocolate Cake 147	Chocolate Chess Pie 167
Dirt Cake 148	Chess Pie............... 168
Fresh Apple Cake 150	Pecan Pie............... 169
Fruit Cocktail Cake...... 151	Apple Crunch Pie 170
Gooey Butter Cake 152	Banana Split Pie 171
Hawaiian Orange Cake... 153	Carrie's Chocolate Pie 172
Honey Bun Cake........ 154	Chocolate Pie 173
Jam Cake............... 155	Coconut Cream Pie...... 174
Orange Blossom Special Cake 156	Coconut Pie............ 175
	Buttermilk Pie........... 176
Pineapple Cake 157	Japanese Fruit Pie 177
Skillet Cake............ 158	Lemon Icebox Pie 1...... 178
Srawberry Sheet Cake.... 159	Lemon Icebox Pie 2...... 179
Vanilla Wafer Cake 160	Lemon Meringue Pie 180
Pumpkin Roll 161	Lemon Cheesecake Pie ... 181
Quick Fruit Cobbler 162	Lemon Mousse Pie 182

Cherry Cheesecake 183	Date Nut Balls. 199
Peanut Butter Pie. 184	Divinity Candy 200
Strawberry Pie 1 185	Peanut Butter Balls 201
Strawberry Pie 2 186	Marcille's Nutty
Brown Sugar Brownies . . . 187	Fudge Candy. 202
Brownies 188	Creamy Pralines 203
Pumpkin Pie Bars 189	Peach Ice Cream 204
Pumpkin Cheesecake Bars 190	Ice Cream 205
Death-by-Caramel Squares 191	Cherry Supreme Dessert . . 206
	Strawberry Pizza 207
Tea Cakes 192	Strawberry Trifle 209
Butterfinger Cookies. 193	Quick Fudge Pudding. . . . 211
Hay Stack Cookies 194	Cream Cheese Pastry 213
Sugar Cookies 195	Popcorn Balls. 214
The Cookie Jar Recipe. . . . 196	Caramel Corn 215
Chocolate Oatmeal Cookies 198	Chocolate Gravy 216
	Chocolate Rolls 217

Helpful Hints 220

History. 227
A Brief History of Mt. Wesley Akin Nazarene Church
1878—2011 (133 Years)

Where to find it in the Bible 243

HEALING FOODS OF THE BIBLE

The Scripture and your diet

Barley
Deuteronomy 8:7-9
"For the LORD your God is bringing you into a good land—a land with streams and pools of water, with springs flowing in the valleys and hills; ⁸a land with wheat and barley, vines and fig trees, pomegranates, olive oil and honey; ⁹a land where bread will not be scarce and you will lack nothing; a land where the rocks are iron and you can dig copper out of the hills."

Beans
Ezekiel 4:9
"Take wheat and barley, beans and lentils, millet and spelt; put them in a storage jar and use them to make bread for yourself. You are to eat it during the 390 days you lie on your side."

2 Samuel 17:28–29
"...brought bedding and bowls and articles of pottery. They also brought wheat and barley, flour and roasted grain, beans and lentils, ²⁹honey and curds, sheep, and cheese from cows' milk

for David and his people to eat. For they said, 'The people have become hungry and tired and thirsty in the desert.'"

Bread
Ezekiel 4:9
See "Beans."

Dairy
Isaiah 7:15, 22
"He will eat curds and honey when he knows enough to reject the wrong and choose the right. [22]And because of the abundance of the milk they give, he will have curds to eat. All who remain in the land will eat curds and honey."

Proverbs 27:27
"You will have plenty of goats' milk to feed you and your family and to nourish your servant girls."

Figs
1 Samuel 30:11–12
"They found an Egyptian in a field and brought him to David. They gave him water to drink and food to eat—[12]part of a cake of pressed figs and two cakes of raisins. He ate and was revived, for he had not eaten any food or drunk any water for three days and three nights."

Fish
Leviticus 11:9–12
"Of all the creatures living in the water of the seas and the streams, you may eat any that have fins and scales. [10]But all creatures in the seas or streams that do not have fins and scales—whether among all the swarming things or among all the other living creatures in the water—you are to detest. [11]And since you are to detest them, you must not eat their meat and you must detest their carcasses. [12]Anything living in the water that does not have fins and scales is to be detestable to you."

Deuteronomy 14:9
"Of all the creatures living in the water, you may eat any that has fins and scales."

Luke 24:42–43
"They gave him a piece of broiled fish, [3]and he took it and ate it in their presence."

Fruit
Ezekiel 47:12
"Fruit trees of all kinds will grow on both banks of the river. Their leaves will not wither, nor will their fruit fail. Every month they will bear, because the water from the sanctuary flows to them. Their fruit will serve for food and their leaves for healing."

Deuteronomy 8:7
"For the LORD your God is bringing you into a good land—a land with streams and pools of water, with springs flowing in the valleys and hills; [8]a land with wheat and barley, vines and fig trees, pomegranates, olive oil and honey; [9]a land where bread will not be scarce and you will lack nothing; a land where the rocks are iron and you can dig copper out of the hills."

Song of Solomon 2:5
"Strengthen me with raisins, refresh me with apples, for I am faint with love."

Garlic
Numbers 11:5
"We remember the fish we ate in Egypt at no cost—also the cucumbers, melons, leeks, onions and garlic."

Grains
Ezekiel 4:9
See "Beans."

Grapes
Numbers 13:23
"When they reached the Valley of Eshcol,[1] they cut off a branch bearing a single cluster of grapes. Two of them carried it on a pole between them, along with some pomegranates and figs."

Genesis 9:20
"Noah, a man of the soil, proceeded to plant a vineyard."

1 Timothy 5:23
"Stop drinking only water, and use a little wine because of your stomach and your frequent illnesses."

1 Kings 21:2
"Ahab said to Naboth, 'Let me have your vineyard to use for a vegetable garden, since it is close to my palace. In exchange I will give you a better vineyard or, if you prefer, I will pay you whatever it is worth.'"

Herbs

Numbers 11:7-9
"The manna was like coriander seed and looked like resin. ⁸The people went around gathering it, and then ground it in a handmill or crushed it in a mortar. They cooked it in a pot or made it into cakes. And it tasted like something made with olive oil. ⁹When the dew settled on the camp at night, the manna also came down."

Psalm 51:7
"Cleanse me with hyssop, and I will be clean; wash me, and I will be whiter than snow."

John 19:29-30
"A jar of wine vinegar was there, so they soaked a sponge in it, put the sponge on a stalk of the hyssop plant, and lifted it to Jesus' lips. ³⁰When he had received the drink, Jesus said, 'It is finished.' With that, he bowed his head and gave up his spirit."

Honey
1 Samuel 14:27
"But Jonathan had not heard that his father had bound the people with the oath, so he reached out the end of the staff that was in his hand and dipped it into the honeycomb. He raised his hand to his mouth, and his eyes brightened."

2 Samuel 17:29
"...honey and curds, sheep, and cheese from cows' milk for David and his people to eat. For they said, 'The people have become hungry and tired and thirsty in the desert.' "

Genesis 43:11
"Then their father Israel said to them, 'If it must be, then do this: Put some of the best products of the land in your bags and take them down to the man as a gift—a little balm and a little honey, some spices and myrrh, some pistachio nuts and almonds.' "

Meat
Genesis 9:3
"Everything that lives and moves will be food for you. Just as I gave you the green plants, I now give you everything."

Leviticus 72:22–27
"The LORD said to Moses, 23'Say to the Israelites: "Do not eat any of the fat of cattle, sheep or goats. 24The fat of an animal found dead or torn by wild animals may be used for any other purpose, but you must not eat it. 25Anyone who eats the fat of an animal from which an offering by fire may be made to the LORD must be cut off from his people. 26And wherever you live, you must not eat the blood of any bird or animal. 27If anyone eats blood, that person must be cut off from his people."' "

Leviticus 3:17
" 'This is a lasting ordinance for the generations to come, wherever you live: You must not eat any fat or any blood.' "

Melon
Numbers 11:5
See "Garlic."

Isaiah 1:8
"The Daughter of Zion is left like a shelter in a vineyard, like a hut in a field of melons, like a city under siege."

Milk
Exodus 3:8
"So I have come down to rescue them from the hand of the Egyptians and to bring them up out of that land into a good and spacious land, a land flowing with milk and honey—the home of the Canaanites, Hittites, Amorites, Perizzites, Hivites and Jebusites."

Isaiah 7:22
"And because of the abundance of the milk they give, he will have curds to eat. All who remain in the land will eat curds and honey."

2 Samuel 17:29
"...honey and curds, sheep, and cheese from cows' milk for David and his people to eat. For they said, 'The people have become hungry and tired and thirsty in the desert.'"

Nuts
Genesis 43:11
See "Honey."

Olives
James 5:14
"Is any one of you sick? He should call the elders of the church to pray over him and anoint him with oil in the name of the Lord."

2 Kings 18:32
"...until I come and take you to a land like your own, a land of grain and new wine, a land of bread and vineyards, a land of olive trees and honey. Choose life and not death! 'Do not listen to Hezekiah, for he is misleading you when he says, "The LORD will deliver us." ' "

Onions
Numbers 11:5
See "Garlic."

Pomegranates
Deuteronomy 8:8
"...a land with wheat and barley, vines and fig trees, pomegranates, olive oil and honey;"

Spices
Matthew 23:23
"Woe to you, teachers of the law and Pharisees, you hypocrites! You give a tenth of your spices—mint, dill and cummin. But you have neglected the more important matters of the law—justice,

mercy and faithfulness. You should have practiced the latter, without neglecting the former."

Luke 11:42
"Woe to you Pharisees, because you give God a tenth of your mint, rue and all other kinds of garden herbs, but you neglect justice and the love of God. You should have practiced the latter without leaving the former undone."

Vegetables
Daniel 1:12–17
"Please test your servants for ten days: Give us nothing but vegetables to eat and water to drink. ¹³Then compare our appearance with that of the young men who eat the royal food, and treat your servants in accordance with what you see."
¹⁴So he agreed to this and tested them for ten days. ¹⁵At the end of the ten days they looked healthier and better nourished than any of the young men who ate the royal food. ¹⁶So the guard took away their choice food and the wine they were to drink and gave them vegetables instead. ¹⁷To these four young men God gave knowledge and understanding of all kinds of literature and learning. And Daniel could understand visions and dreams of all kinds."

Numbers 11:5
See "Garlic."

Ezekiel 4:9
See "Beans."

Genesis 1:11
"Then God said, 'Let the land produce vegetation: seed-bearing plants and trees on the land that bear fruit with seed in it, according to their various kinds.' And it was so."

Genesis 1:29
"Then God said, 'I give you every seed-bearing plant on the face of the whole earth and every tree that has fruit with seed in it. They will be yours for food.'"

Wheat
Jeremiah 41:8
"But ten of them said to Ishmael, 'Don't kill us! We have wheat and barley, oil and honey, hidden in a field.' So he let them alone and did not kill them with the others."

Ezekiel 4:9
See "Beans."

Yogurt (curds)
2 Samuel 17:28-29
"...brought bedding and bowls and articles of pottery. They also brought wheat and barley, flour and roasted grain, beans and

lentils, ²⁹honey and curds, sheep, and cheese from cows' milk for David and his people to eat. For they said, 'The people have become hungry and tired and thirsty in the desert.' "

HEALING CHECKLIST

Six things to contemplate and act on.

1. Prayer. It's just common sense that you're not likely to get something unless you ask for it. Jesus told his disciples to pray night and day and not to give up. He also told us to have the elders of the church pray for us.

James 5:14–15
"Is any one of you sick? He should call the elders of the church to pray over him and anoint him with oil in the name of the Lord. ¹⁵And the prayer offered in faith will make the sick person well; the Lord will raise him up. If he has sinned, he will be forgiven."

Luke 18:1–7
"¹Then Jesus told his disciples a parable to show them that they should always pray and not give up. ²He said: 'In a certain town there was a judge who neither feared God nor cared about men. ³And there was a widow in that town who kept coming to him with the plea, "Grant me justice against my adversary." ⁴For some time he refused. But finally he said to himself, "Even though I don't fear God or care about men, ⁵yet because this widow keeps bothering me, I will see that she gets justice, so that she won't eventually wear me out with her coming!" ⁶And the Lord said,

"Listen to what the unjust judge says." ' ⁷And will not God bring about justice for his chosen ones, who cry out to him day and night? Will he keep putting them off?"

James 5:16
"Therefore confess your sins to each other and pray for each other so that you may be healed. The prayer of a righteous man is powerful and effective."

Matthew 18:19–20
"Again, I tell you that if two of you on earth agree about anything you ask for, it will be done for you by my Father in heaven. ²⁰For where two or three come together in my name, there am I with them."

2. Faith. While a great amount of faith is not required for God to heal, it certainly can't hurt. Jesus was unable to do miracles in his hometown because of the lack of faith but he was still able to heal sick people! With faith, Jesus tells us that, "Nothing will be impossible for you."

Mark 6:1–6
"¹Jesus left there and went to his hometown, accompanied by his disciples. ²When the Sabbath came, he began to teach in the synagogue, and many who heard him were amazed. 'Where did this man get these things?' they asked. 'What's this wisdom that

has been given him, that he even does miracles! ³Isn't this the carpenter? Isn't this Mary's son and the brother of James, Joseph, Judas and Simon? Aren't his sisters here with us?' And they took offense at him. ⁴Jesus said to them, 'Only in his hometown, among his relatives and in his own house is a prophet without honor.' ⁵He could not do any miracles there, except lay his hands on a few sick people and heal them. ⁶And he was amazed at their lack of faith. Then Jesus went around teaching from village to village."

Matthew 17:19
"...when he said 'I tell you the truth, if you have faith as small as a mustard seed, you can say to this mountain, "Move from here to there" and it will move. Nothing will be impossible for you.' "

3. Love & Forgiveness. There is no question that God wants us to love and forgive each other. Love is God's command. Love is healing.

John 15:12–14
"My command is this: Love each other as I have loved you. ¹³Greater love has no one than this, that he lay down his life for his friends. ¹⁴You are my friends if you do what I command."

Hebrews 13:1–2
"Keep on loving each other as brothers. ²Do not forget to entertain strangers, for by so doing some people have entertained angels without knowing it."

Isaiah 58:7–8
"Is it not to share your food with the hungry and to provide the poor wanderer with shelter—when you see the naked, to clothe him, and not to turn away from your own flesh and blood? ⁸Then your light will break forth like the dawn, and your healing will quickly appear; then your righteousness will go before you, and the glory of the LORD will be your rear guard."

1 Corinthians 13:4–7
"Love is patient, love is kind. It does not envy, it does not boast, it is not proud. ⁵It is not rude, it is not self-seeking, it is not easily angered, it keeps no record of wrongs. ⁶Love does not delight in evil but rejoices with the truth. ⁷It always protects, always trusts, always hopes, always perseveres."

Mark 11:23-25
"I tell you the truth, if anyone says to this mountain, 'Go, throw yourself into the sea,' and does not doubt in his heart but believes that what he says will happen, it will be done for him. ²⁴Therefore I tell you, whatever you ask for in prayer, believe that you have received it, and it will be yours. ²⁵And when you stand

praying, if you hold anything against anyone, forgive him, so that your Father in heaven may forgive you your sins."

Proverbs 15:30
"A cheerful look brings joy to the heart, and good news gives health to the bones."

Proverbs 12:18
"Reckless words pierce like a sword, but the tongue of the wise brings healing.

Proverbs 16:24
"Pleasant words are a honeycomb, sweet to the soul and healing to the bones."

4. God's Protection. There are forces of evil from which you may need protection. Ask God for protection.

Ephesians 6:11–13
"[11]Put on the full armor of God so that you can take your stand against the devil's schemes. [12]For our struggle is not against flesh and blood, but against the rulers, against the authorities, against the powers of this dark world and against the spiritual forces of evil in the heavenly realms. [13]Therefore put on the full armor of God, so that when the day of evil comes, you may be able to stand your ground, and after you have done everything, to stand."

5. Good Medical Care. God works his miracles in many ways and through many people. Today's medical community has a lot to offer and with God's grace can save your life.

Luke 5:31
"Jesus answered them, 'It is not the healthy who need a doctor, but the sick.' "

6. A healthy diet. There are many references in the Bible about what we should and shouldn't eat. Today's "Mediterranean Diet" follows biblical references.

Ezekiel 47:12
"Fruit trees of all kinds will grow on both banks of the river. Their leaves will not wither, nor will their fruit fail. Every month they will bear, because the water from the sanctuary flows to them. Their fruit will serve for food and their leaves for healing."

Help yourself!
There's always plenty to eat
at a Mt. Wesley Akin lunch.

APPETIZERS AND BEVERAGES

TURNING THANKS

Baked Corn Dip

Gina Dodson Griggs

[5]"We remember the fish we ate in Egypt at no cost, also the cucumbers, melons, leeks, onions and garlic. [6]But now we have lost our appetite; we never see anything but this manna!"

Numbers 11:5-6

Ingredients

- 2   11 oz. cans mexicorn, drained
- 1   2 oz. jar pimientos 2, drained
- 1   bunch green onions chopped
- ¼   cup jalapenos, chopped
- 1½   cup sour cream
- 1   cup mayonnaise
- 1   teaspoon garlic powder
- 1   teaspoon Accent seasoning
- 1   pound grated cheese, sharp or colby jack blend

Instructions

Preheat oven to 350 degrees. Spray 9 x 13" pan with cooking oil spray.

Mix all ingredients together and pour into pan.

Bake for 15 minutes, stir and bake for another 15 minutes.

Serve hot with tortilla chips or corn chips.

APPETIZERS

Possum Dip

Jerry Walters

Ingredients

- 2 lbs. ground beef (or 1 possum) browned and drained
- 2 16 oz. cans ranch style beans
- 1 can large Rotel tomatoes with chilis
- 1 medium onion, chopped
- 2 lbs. mexican Velveeta cheese
- ½ cup milk
- salt and pepper to taste

Instructions

Cook in a crock pot.

Serve with corn chips as scoops.

TURNING THANKS

Sausage Balls

Jerry Walters

Ingredients
1 lb. sausage
1 cup cheddar cheese
2 cups Bisquick

Instructions
Mix all ingredients and roll into 1" balls.

Bake at 425 degrees for 15 minutes.

Mt. Wesley Akin started out as Mt. Wesley Methodist. Many of the Methodist church members remained in attendance at Mt. Wesley Nazarene, though some did not transfer their membership.

Two known attendees were Jerome R. Vestal and Mrs. Rose Anna Adams Vestal.

Rose Anna Adams Vestal is Jerry's grandmother.

APPETIZERS

Sausage Cheese Dip

Robbie Fox

Ingredients
- 2 lbs. Velveeta cheese
- 1½ lbs. sausage
- 2 cans Rotel tomatoes

Instructions
Brown sausage and drain. Drain Rotel tomatoes. Cut Velveeta cheese in cubes and put in a crockpot. Add the drained sausage and tomatoes. Stir until melted.

Serve with tortilla chips or corn chips.

The followers of Jesus were initially called "Nazarenes" (Acts 24:5), a term perhaps used by Jesus himself; hence the Church of the Nazarene.

TURNING THANKS

Pineapple Cheese Ball

Frances Haywood Woodall Fraser

Ingredients

- 2 8 oz. packages of cream cheese, softened
- 1 can pineapple, small, drained
- ½–1 cup pecans
- ¼ cup green peppers, finely chopped
- 2 tablespoons onions, finely chopped
- 1 teaspoon seasoned salt

Instructions

Beat cream cheese until smooth, add pineapple, ½ of the pecans, pepper, onion and salt.

Blend and shape into balls. Roll in the remaining pecans and chill.

BEVERAGES

Frances' Punch

Frances Haywood Woodall Fraser

Ingredients
1	quart grape juice	1	bottle Sundrop, 2 liter
1	quart apple juice		

Instructions
Mix together and chill.

Can substitute ½ gallon cranberry juice for the Sundrop.

Miss Frances is third from left, in the plaid dress.

TURNING THANKS

Banana Crush Punch

Shirley Hanback

"Then he took a cup, and when he had given thanks, he gave it to them, and they all drank from it."

Mark 14:23

Ingredients

- 3 bananas
- 1 6 oz. can frozen lemonade, thawed, undiluted
- 3 quarts Sprite
- 1 12 oz. can frozen orange juice concentrate
- 3 cups water
- 2 cups sugar

Instructions

Combine banana and lemonade in a blender until smooth.

Mix in other ingredients and freeze until ready to serve.

BEVERAGES

Orange Punch

Marie Vestal Walters

Ingredients
- 2   2 liter bottles Gingerale or Sundrop
- 1   large can pineapple juice
- 1   quart or ½ gallon orange sherbert

Instructions
Mix liquids in punch bowl and float dollops of sherbert on top.

TURNING THANKS

Lemon Punch

Marie Vestal Walters

Ingredients

1   gallon lemonade
2   large cans pineapple juice
2   2 liter bottles Gingerale or Sundrop
    Orange sherbert

Instructions

Mix liquids in punch bowl and float dollops of sherbert on top. You can color this and use any kind of sherbert.

Akin Chapel members, 1918

BEVERAGES

MaMa's Christmas Punch

Marylin Williams Peach

Ingredients

1	quart grape juice	1	pint pineapple juice
1	cup orange juice	2	cups sugar
1	cup lemon juice	2	quarts ginger ale or 7-UP

Instructions
Mix all the juices.

Just before serving, add ice and 2 quarts of ginger ale or 7-UP.

TURNING THANKS

Hot Cranberry Tea

Ramona Robertson

Ingredients
Mix together in large coffeepot:

1	quart apple juice	1	6 oz. can frozen orange juice concentrate
1	quart cranberry juice	1	gallon water
1	cup lemon juice	3	cups sugar
		1	small box cherry Jell-O

Put in basket of coffee pot:

4	family-size tea bags	3	teaspoons whole cloves
4	cinnamon sticks		

Instructions
Turn on coffeepot and perk. Makes approximately 50 cups.
I halve the recipe to use in 30 cup percolator.

BEVERAGES

Dutch Oven Hot Cider

Ramona Robertson

Ingredients

- 1 cup water
- ½ cup sugar
- 2 cinnamon sticks
- 4 whole allspice or ½ teaspoon ground allspice
- ½ teaspoon ground ginger
- 4 cups apple cider
- 2 cups orange juice
- ¼ cup lemon juice

Instructions

Bring water and sugar to a boil in a small saucepan over medium heat, stirring constantly. Boil 3 minutes.

Add cinnamon, allspice, and ginger; reduce heat and simmer for 10 minutes, stirring occasionally.

Pour mixture into a Dutch oven and add cider and juices; bring to a boil. Serve hot.

Yield: About 7 cups

TURNING THANKS

Boiled Custard

Gail Pigg

Ingredients

½	gallon sweet milk	6	each whole eggs
1¾	cups sugar	1	tablespoon vanilla

Instructions

Beat eggs thoroughly.

Add the remining ingredients. Cook in a heavy pan allowing it come to a boil, stirring often.

When done, the custard coats the spoon, feels thick when stirred, and the foam disappears.

NOTES

NOTES

Around the corner from Mt. Wesley Church was the Mt. Wesley School House, which was built around 1878.

NOTES

Mt. Wesley school, 1912

It isn't lunch without rolls, biscuits and cornbread!

BREADS

TURNING THANKS

"Red Lobster" Biscuits

Carol Walters

"Because there is one loaf, we, who are many, are one body, for we all share the one loaf."

1 Corinthians 10:17

Ingredients
- 2 cups Bisquick Baking Mix
- ⅔ cup milk
- ½ cup shredded cheddar cheese
- ¼ cup butter or margarine (melted)
- ¼ teaspoon garlic powder

Instructions
Preheat oven to 450 degrees. Mix Bisquick, milk, and cheese in a bowl. Using a tablespoon, drop dough onto ungreased cookie sheet. Bake 8-10 minutes until golden brown.

Mix margarine and garlic powder. Brush mixture over hot biscuits before serving. Makes 10-12 biscuits.

BREADS

Homemade Biscuits

Noma Jean Dodson

Ingredients
- 3 cups White Lily self-rising flour
- 1 cup Field lard
- ¾ cup milk
- ¾ cup buttermilk

Instructions
Sift flour into a large bowl. Add lard, milk, and buttermilk. Mix by hand.

Generously flour a smooth surface and roll out the dough to about ½" thick.

Cut with a medium-sized biscuit cutter.

Place on a greased sheet pan and bake at 450 degrees until golden brown.

These biscuits freeze very well. Put the cut dough on a cookie sheet and freeze. Once frozen, place in freezer bags.

TURNING THANKS

Hawaiian Sweet Rolls
Noma Jean Dodson

"Then Jacob gave Esau some bread and some lentil stew. He ate and drank, and then got up and left. So Esau despised his birthright."

Genesis 25:34

Ingredients

6½–7 cups all-purpose flour	1 cup milk
¾ cup mashed potato flakes	½ cup water
⅔ cup sugar	½ cup margarine or butter
1 teaspoon salt	1 cup pineapple juice, room temperature
½ teaspoon ginger	
2 teaspoons vanilla	3 eggs
2 packages active dry yeast	

Instructions

Combine 3 cups flour, mashed potato flakes, sugar, salt, ginger, vanilla, and yeast.

In a sauce pan, heat the milk, water, and margarine until very warm (120–130 degrees).

Add warm liquid, pineapple juice, and eggs to the flour mixture. Blend at low speed until moistened. Beat 4 minutes at medium speed.

BREADS

By hand, stir in 3 cups of flour to form a stiff dough.

On a floured surface, knead in ½ to 1 cup of flour until smooth and elastic. Place dough in a greased bowl and cover loosely with plastic wrap and a cloth towel. Let rise in a warm place until dough is light and doubled in size, about 1 to 1½ hours. Punch dough down and roll out on a floured surface. Cut with a biscuit cutter and place on a greased baking sheet.

Brush with egg white and a small amount of water. Cover with a cloth towel and let rise until rolls are doubled in size.

Bake at 375 degrees until done.

J. R. Vestal (Jerome) is the grandfather of current member Marie Vestal Walters. Noma Jean Dodson is the daughter of Marie Vestal Walters.

TURNING THANKS

Quick Rolls

Sharon Sisk in Memory of Louise Dodson

Ingredients
- 1½ sticks butter, melted
- 1 package yeast in 2 cups of very warm water
- 4 cups self-rising flour
- ⅓ cup sugar

Instructions
Add liquid ingredients to dry and mix with mixer about 2 minutes.

Spoon into a greased muffin pan and bake for 20 minutes at 400 degrees.

Makes 2 dozen.

BREADS

Louise's Spoon Rolls

Kimberly Kelley

"Elijah said to her, 'Don't be afraid. Go home and do as you have said. But first make a small loaf of bread for me from what you have and bring it to me, and then make something for yourself and your son. For this is what the LORD, the God of Israel, says: "The jar of flour will not be used up and the jug of oil will not run dry until the day the LORD sends rain on the land." ' "

1 Kings 17:12

Ingredients

1	package dry yeast	¾	cup melted shortening, vegetable oil or canola oil
2	cups lukewarm water		
4	cups self-rising flour		
¼	cup sugar	1	egg

Instructions

Dissolve yeast in the warm water. Mix together all other ingredients. Store in a covered container and use as desired.

To cook, spoon the batter into well-greased muffin tins and bake at 425 degrees for 20 minutes. There is no need to let the rolls rise before baking.

TURNING THANKS

One Hour Rolls

Marie Vestal Walters

Ingredients

2	cups flour	1	package yeast
¼	cup shortening	¼	cup warm water
2	tablespoons sugar	¾	cup buttermilk

Instructions

Dissolve yeast in warm water. Mix flour and sugar.

Cut shortening into flour mixture, then add yeast and buttermilk, working the mixture into dough.

On a floured surface, roll dough to about ¼-inch thick and cut out rolls with biscuit cutter.

Place rolls in greased pan and let rise 1 hour. Bake at 425 degrees.

BREADS

Dinner Rolls

Agnes Williams

Ingredients

2	tablespoons soft shortening	2	tablespoons sugar
1	package active dry yeast	1	teaspoon salt
1	cup warm water, not hot	2½	cups plain flour
		1	egg

Instructions

In large bowl with cover, dissolve yeast in warm water. Stir in sugar, salt, and half the flour. Beat until smooth. Add egg and shortening. Beat in remaining flour till smooth. Scrape down sides of bowl.

Seal and let stand in warm place until dough is doubled in size.

Punch down dough. Turn out on pastry board or wax paper. Press down flat. Cut with cutter.

Place on cookie sheet. Let rise again. Brush with melted butter.

Bake in preheated oven at 400 degrees.

TURNING THANKS

Corn Cornbread

Jim Hanback

"At that time Jesus went on the Sabbath day through the corn; and his disciples were an hungered, and began to pluck the ears of corn and to eat."

Matthew 12:1 KJV

Ingredients

- 2 cups cornmeal
- 2 large eggs
- 1 15 oz. can cream style corn
- ½ cup shortening
- 1 cup buttermilk (more or less as needed to liquify)

Instructions

Mix the cornmeal, eggs, and corn together until thoroughly blended. Add buttermilk to the mix until it becomes liquid enough to pour into the skillet. Allow the mix to rest while the skillet preheats.

Place the shortening in a seasoned cast iron skillet and put in oven to pre-heat at 350 F. It helps to spray the skillet with canola oil prior to the shortening. Leave the skillet in the oven until all shortening is melted and thoroughly hot.

Pour the melted shortening into the batter mix and blend thoroughly. Leave a slight skim of the melted shortening in the skillet. The mix should sizzle when the shortening is added if the shortening is hot enough.

BREADS

Pour the mix into the skillet and place in the 350 F. oven for 45 minutes to an hour. Baking time depends on the oven. To keep the bread moist, observe occassionally and remove when the top has turned a light golden brown.

The old church sign still sits out back.

TURNING THANKS

Zucchini Bread

Marie Vestal Walters

Ingredients

3	eggs (well beaten)	1	teaspoon salt
2	cups sugar	1	teaspoon soda
1	cup oil	¼	teaspoon baking powder
2	cups grated zucchini	3	cups flour
1 teaspoon cinnamon		1	cup chopped pecans

Instructions

Mix dry ingredients together and set aside.

Cream sugar and oil together, then add beaten eggs and zucchini.

Add dry ingredients.

Pour batter into 2 greased and floured load pans. Bake for 1 hour at 350 degrees. Use a toothpick to test for doneness.

Cool in pans for 10 minutes. Remove from pans and cool on a wire rack.

Freezes well.

BREADS

Banana Bread 1

Robbie Fox

"Then he gave a loaf of bread, a cake of dates and a cake of raisins to each person in the whole crowd of Israelites, both men and women. And all the people went to their homes."

2 Samuel 6:19

Ingredients

1	cup sugar	½	cup chopped nuts
½	cup oil	1	cup self-rising flour
2	bananas, mashed	1	teaspoon vanilla
2	eggs		

Instructions

Cream sugar and oil. Add eggs, bananas, and vanilla. Stir in flour, then add nuts.

Bake in a greased and floured loaf pan at 350 degees for 35–40 minutes.

[Handwritten note: The 7 Super foods of the Bible: wheat, barley, grapes, figs, pomegranate, olive oil, honey]

TURNING THANKS

Banana Bread 2

Sharon Sisk in Memory of Buddy and Elizabeth Dodson

Ingredients

1	cup sugar	2	bananas
2	eggs	2	cup self-rising flour
1	stick butter	½	cup nuts

Instructions

Cream together sugar, eggs and butter. Add bananas, flour and nuts.

Bake in a loaf pan at 350 degrees for 1 hour.

Sharon is the granddaughter of Akin Church founder J. M. Dodson.

BREADS

Banana Bread 3

Sarah Williams

"Then the LORD said to Moses, 'Take the following fine spices: 500 shekels of liquid myrrh, half as much (that is, 250 shekels) of fragrant cinnamon, 250 shekels of fragrant calamus.'"

Exodus 30:22-23

Ingredients

1	cup self-rising flour	½	cup oil
1	cup sugar	1	teaspoon vanilla
1	teaspoon cinnamon	2	bananas, large, mashed
½	teaspoon pumpkin spice	½	cup chopped nuts, optional
½	teaspoon ginger		
2	eggs		

Instructions

Sift flour and all dry ingredients together. Mix in all other ingredients.

Spoon into greased loaf pan and bake at 350 degrees for 35–40 minutes or until it tests done. Let cool before removing from pan.

TURNING THANKS

Ginger Bread

Marie Vestal Walters

Ingredients

¼	cup butter	1¾	cup flour
½	cup sugar	1	teaspoon ginger
½	cup molasses	½	teaspoon cinnamon
1	egg	½	teaspoon baking soda
½	cup buttermilk	½	teaspoon salt

Instructions

Cream butter and sugar. Add molasses and milk.

Mix together dry ingredients and sift into the other mix. Blend well.

Bake at 350 degrees until done.

This is from a 1949 cookbook that Marie used when "Dinner on the Ground" at the church meant exactly that.

There was no kitchen or fellowship hall, so you ate on the ground picnic style.

BREADS

Breakfast Pizza

Robbie Fox

Ingredients

1	lb. pork sausage	6	eggs
1	can crescent rolls	½	cup milk
1	lb. cheese, grated (½ lb. each mozzarella and cheddar)	1	teaspoon oregano (optional) salt and pepper to taste

Instructions

Crumble sausage in a skillet and fry until done, but not hard. Drain. Spray a baking pan, 13 x 9 x 2, with cooking spray and unroll the crescent rolls in the pan in 2-inch strips. Pinch together the seams and perforated places. Spread with fingers to cover the bottom of the pan.

Crumble sausage over the rolls evenly. Sprinkle cheese over sausage. Mix eggs, milk, salt, and oregano together and pour over the cheese as evenly as possible.

Bake in a 350 degree oven for 30–35 minutes. Let stand for 5 or 10 minutes, cut into squares, and serve hot.

NOTES

NOTES

Rocks and stones from the original
Akin Chapel Nazarene Church
were salvaged after it was torn down
for the Natchez Trace.
  The materials were moved to
        Camp Garner Creek.

In the old days,
everyone canned fresh vegetables
from the garden.

PRESERVES

TURNING THANKS

Catfish Campus Tomato Pickle

Jerry Walters

"Then he took the seven loaves and the fish, and when he had given thanks, he broke them and gave them to the disciples, and they in turn to the people.

Matthew 15:36

Ingredients

4	quarts green tomatoes and onions, quartered	1	tablespoon salt
2	cups sugar	1	tablespoon pickling spice wrapped in gauze
2	cups vinegar		

Instructions

Mix all ingredients together and bring to a boil.

Put in sterilized jars and seal.

PRESERVES

Catfish Relish

Betty Hay by Janie Fox

Ingredients

2	gallons chopped green tomatoes (about 12 pounds)	½	quart jalapeno peppers
		6	cups sugar
		1	red sweet pepper
½	gallon chopped onions (about 3 pounds)	1	quart vinegar
		2	tablespoons salt
2	large celery stalks		

Instructions

Mix all together and boil 10 minutes.

Put in canning jars and seal.

Betty, along with husband J. W. and sons Mickey and Kenny, attended our church in the 1970s and 80s.

TURNING THANKS

Corn Relish

Liz Shouse Brunson

Ingredients

1	can white corn niblets		1	onion, chopped
1	can yellow corn niblets		2	stalks celery, chopped
1	cup red peppers, diced		1	cup sugar
1	cup green peppers, diced		1	cup vinegar

Instructions

Mix all the chopped vegetables together.

Bring sugar and vinegar to a boil.

Pour over the vegetable mixture.

PRESERVES

Aunt Ola's Closet Pickles

Norma Jones

"At mealtime Boaz said to her, 'Come over here. Have some bread and dip it in the wine vinegar.' When she sat down with the harvesters, he offered her some roasted grain. She ate all she wanted and had some left over." *Ruth 2:14*

Ingredients

- enough cucumbers to fill a gallon jug
- 2-3 drops oil of cloves
- 4 lbs. sugar
- distilled vinegar to cover

Instructions

Wash cucumbers and place whole in a wide-mouth gallon jug. Cover with vinegar.

Place jug in a paper sack and set in closet for 6 weeks.

Pour vinegar down the drain. Cut cucumbers into pickle slices. Layer the slices back in the jug with a layer of sugar over each layer of pickles. Add the oil of cloves.

Seal and place back in closet for one week. Shake to make sure all sugar is dissolved.

Put in pint jars or leave in gallon.

TURNING THANKS

Pickled Beets

Jerry Walters

Ingredients

15–20	beets, fresh	½	cup water
2	cups vinegar	1	tablespoon salt
2	cups sugar	1	tablespoon pickling spice

Instructions

Cut tops of beets off leaving a 1" stem. Leave the roots.

Boil beets in water until tender and skin loosens.

Mix all other ingrdients. Place beets and mix in a large pan.

Bring to a boil and then place in jars.

PRESERVES

Christmas Jam

Ramona Robertson

Ingredients

- 1 8 oz. jar maraschino cherries (you can use 4 oz. red and 4 oz. green)
- 1 11 oz. package dried apricots
- 3½ cups water
- 6 cups sugar
- 1 13 oz. can pineapple chunks, drained

Instructions

Drain cherries; reserve juice.

Combine water, cherry juice, and apricots in a large pot; allow mixture to stand for one hour.

Cook over low heat until apricots are tender.

Add sugar. Cook, stirring frequently, until thick and clear.

Cut cherries into fourths and add to mixture along with pineapple. Cook for 5 minutes more, stirring frequently.

Pour into pint jars and seal. Makes approximately 6½ pints.

TURNING THANKS

Pear Honey

Norma Jones

"If you find honey, eat just enough."

Proverbs 25:16

Ingredients

12-14	pears, medium, ripe, peeled and cored	1	20 oz. can crushed pineapple, undrained
8	cups sugar	3	tablespoons lemon juice

Instructions

Puree the pears in a food processor or blender; pour into a large kettle or dutch oven.

Add remaining ingredients; bring to a boil.

Reduce heat, cook and stir, uncovered, for 50–60 minutes or until thickened.

Remove from heat. Pour into hot jars, leaving ¼-inch head space.

Adjust the caps. Process for 20 minutes in a boiling water bath.

Makes 12 half-pints.

NOTES

NOTES

The new Fellowship Hall being built!

NOTES

The salads and sides are always a big hit at church lunches!

SOUPS AND SALADS

TURNING THANKS

Chili with Tomato

Jim Hanback

Ingredients

2	tablespoons oil	½	teaspoon pepper
1	lb. lean ground beef	½	teaspoon sugar
1	large onion, chopped	1	teaspoon chili powder (or to taste)
2	cloves garlic, minced		
1	27 oz. can chili beans, undrained (mild or hot)	½	cup ketchup
		1	8 oz. can tomato sauce
2	cups water	1	27 oz. can petite diced tomatoes
½	teaspoon salt		

Instructions

Heat oil in a skillet and cook beef until lighty browned. Drain excess fat. Place the meat in a large pot.

Cook the onion and garlic until soft. Mix the onion, garlic, and all other ingredients in the pot with the meat. Stir thoroughly.

Place on high heat until it starts to bubble. Reduce the heat, cover the pan, and simmer on low 45 minutes to 1 hour.

You can add cayenne pepper or hot sauce to your taste if desired. Ground turkey can also be used.

SOUPS

Vegetable Beef Stew

Audrey Hood

Ingredients

- 2 tablespoons salad oil
- 2 lbs. stewing meat, cut into 1-inch cubes
- ½ cup water
- ½ lb. bacon slices
- 4 onions, sliced
- 1 can stewed tomatoes
- 2 green peppers, thinly sliced
- 1 teaspoon salt
- 1 dash pepper
- hot cooked rice

Instructions

In a large, heavy skillet, heat oil and brown beef on all sides. Drain off excess fat and add water. Cover and cook over low heat 1 ½ hours.

Meanwhile, in a medium skillet, cook bacon until crisp. Cut in 1" pieces and add to beef. Add onion to the bacon fat and cook until tender. Remove and drain and add to beef.

Add the remaining ingredients (except rice) and simmer 15 minutes longer or until meat is tender. Serve over hot rice.

Audrey, her husband Robert Carrol, and their sons Steven and Chuck attended Mt. Wesley until the new highway took their home and they moved away.

TURNING THANKS

Salvation Soup—Vegetarian

Jim Hanback

"Then God said, 'I give you every seed-bearing plant on the face of the whole earth and every tree that has fruit with seed in it. They will be yours for food.'"

Genesis 1:29

Ingredients

- 2 tablespoons olive oil
- 1 28 oz. can tomatoes
- 3 cloves garlic, crushed
- ½ cup dry grain: barley, brown rice, quinoa, etc.
- 3 carrots, sliced and diced
- ½ teaspoon thyme
- 2 teaspoons basil
- 2 teaspoons oregano
- 1 teaspoon sea salt
- 1-2 cups shredded cabbage
- 2 onions, chopped
- 1½ cups beans: kidney, chickpeas or lentils
- 3 stalks celery, sliced and diced
- 2 tablespoons parsley
- 6 cups water (substitute with vegetable broth if desired)

Instructions

Sauté onions and garlic in oil. Add rest of the ingredients and bring to a boil. Reduce heat and simmer for 1 hour, stirring occasionally.

Try adding 1 cup corn or peas, 1 cup green beans, 1 cup chopped onions, 1 small zucchini sliced or 1 potato diced. Use your imagination and add or substitute for your own taste.

SOUPS

Corn Chowder

Marie Vestal Walters

Ingredients

6	slices bacon, cooked crisp	¼	teaspoon pepper
1	cup onion, sautéed	2	15 oz. cans cream style corn
1	cup celery, sautéed		
4	cups potatoes, diced and cooked	1	15 oz. can whole kernel corn
3	tablespoons flour	2	cups milk (added a little at a time)
½	teaspoon salt		

Instructions

Mix all ingredients; heat and serve with corn bread or crackers.

Serves 18 to 20 people.

TURNING THANKS

Seven Layer Salad

Carol Walters

Ingredients

1	head of lettuce, shredded	1	small sweet onion
4	oz. shredded cheddar cheese	1	can green peas (or frozen if preferred)
1	cup diced green pepper	8	slices bacon, cooked crisp

Instructions

Dressing:
Combine 2 cups mayonnaise and 2 tablespoons sugar.

Layer salad in 13 x 9" dish, starting with lettuce, then pepper, sweet onion, peas, dressing, cheese, and sprinkle bacon on top.

Variation: add celery.

SALADS

Broccoli Salad 1

Janie Fox

Ingredients

1	bunch broccoli, chopped	½	cup sunflower seeds, hulled
½	cup red onion, chopped	½	cup raisins
1	cup celery, chopped	¾	cup mayo, for dressing
1	lb. bacon, fried crisp and crumbled	¼	cup sugar, for dressing
		2	tablespoons vinegar

Instructions

Combine the salad ingredients in a large bowl.

Mix the dressing ingredients until the sugar is disolved.

Pour dressing over salad mix and serve chilled.

TURNING THANKS

Broccoli Salad 2

Frances Haywood Woodall Fraser

Ingredients

1	large bunch broccoli, finely chopped	½	cup raisins
		½	cup red onions
½	cup pecans	13	slices bacon, cooked crisp

for dressing:

1	cup mayonnaise	2	tablespoons vinegar
½	cup sugar		

Instructions

Mix together and refrigerate dressing overnight.

Apply dressing to salad just before serving.

Variation: Add finely chopped cauliflower.

SALADS

Broccoli and Cauliflower Salad

Carol Walters

Ingredients

1	large bunch broccoli (raw)	½	cup raisins
1	large head cauliflower	½	cup pecans
½	cup red or white onion, chopped	13	slices bacon, cooked crispy and crumbled

for dressing:

1	cup mayonnaise	1-2	tablespoons vinegar
½	cup sugar or Splenda		(I use less vinegar and add according to taste)

Instructions

Chop raw broccoli and cauliflower, add other ingredients, and mix well.

Cook the bacon and add just before serving. Makes a large bowl.

This will keep for several days in the refrigerator, so it can be fixed the day before to carry for a meal.

TURNING THANKS

Marinated Vegetable Salad

Allene Scott

Ingredients
for salad:

- 1 16 oz. can french-cut green Beans
- 1 16 oz. can small green peas
- 1 12 oz. can shoe peg corn
- 1 green pepper, chopped
- 1 2 oz. jar pimentos
- 1 cup chopped celery
- 1 bunch of green onions, chopped

for marinade:

- ¾ cup vinegar
- ½ cup vegetable oil
- 1 teaspoon salt
- 1 teaspoon pepper
- 1 cup sugar
- 1 tablespoon water

Instructions
for salad:

Drain cans and combine all ingredients. Cover with marinade.

for marinade:

Combine all ingredients and bring to a boil. Pour over vegetables.

Refrigerate 24 hours before serving.

SALADS

Summer Slaw

Reece Robertson

Ingredients

1	large tomato, diced	½	cup sugar
1	medium onion, diced	¼	cup water
1	bell pepper, diced	1	teaspoon salt
1	cucumber, diced	½	teaspoon sesame seed
1	cup vinegar	¼	teaspoon caraway seed

Instructions

Mix all ingredients in non-metal container and refrigerate.

This will keep approximately one month.

Easter 1965

TURNING THANKS

Cabbage Salad

Janie Fox

Ingredients

1	head large cabbage	1	cup salad oil
1	green pepper, sliced paper thin	1	cup sugar
		¾	cup white vinegar
1	medium onion, thin sliced	1½	teaspoon salt
1	medium jar pimento, drained	1	teaspoon celery seed

Instructions

Toss the cabbage, pepper, onion, and pimento in a large bowl.

Mix all other ingredients together and boil for 2 minutes.

Pour the hot dressing over the vegetables, cover tightly.

Refrigerate for 4 hours before serving.

SALADS

Lemon Cabbage Salad

Marie Vestal Walters

Ingredients

6	cups cabbage, shredded	½	cup vinegar
2	medium carrots, grated	½	cup water
¾	cup salad oil	1	cup sugar
1	onion, grated	1	teaspoon salt
1	small green pepper, grated	¾	teaspoon mustard seed
1	3 oz. package lemon Jell-O	1	teaspoon celery seed

Instructions

Combine cabbage, onions, peppers ,and carrots. Add salt, mustard seed, and celery seed.

Heat vinegar, water, and sugar mixture until it boils, then add Jell-O. Stir until cool.

When the vinegar mixture is cool, pour over the cabbage mixture and let stand overnight in the refrigerator.

TURNING THANKS

Buttermilk Salad

Frances Haywood Woodall Fraser

Ingredients
- 1 package peach Jell-O
- 1 carton whipped topping
- 1 16 oz. can crushed pineapple, undrained
- 2 cups buttermilk

Instructions
In a heavy saucepan, mix Jell-O and pineapple. Cook on low heat until Jell-O is completely dissolved.

Place in refrigerator until cool but not beginning to congeal. Remove from refrigerator and add buttermilk. Stir until well blended. Add whipping cream and blend well.

Pour into a 11 x 13" pan or your favorite mold and refrigerate until time to serve.

SALADS

Jell-O Salad
Gail Pigg

Ingredients
- 1 box strawberry Jell-O
- 1 small can crushed pineapple, drained
- 1 small carton cottage cheese
- 1 8 oz. container Cool Whip, thawed

Instructions
Mix dry Jell-O and pineapple together.

Add cottage cheese and Cool Whip.

Mix well and refrigerate.

TURNING THANKS

Orange Salad

In Memory of Marie Hood

Ingredients
1	8 oz. box orange Jell-O	1	cup Cool Whip
1	cup cottage cheese	1	can mandarin oranges

Instructions
Mix all ingredients and garnish with orange halves and pecans.

Marie, husband Buddy, and children David and Gail were early members of the Mt. Wesley Congregation.

SALADS

Pretzel Salad

Sarah Williams

Ingredients

Crust

2	cups pretzels, crushed	¾	cup butter, melted
3	tablespoons sugar		

Filling

1	8 oz. package cream cheese, softened	1	package frozen whipped topping, thawed
		1	cup sugar

Topping

2	cups boiling water		frozen
		2	3 oz. packages strawberry gelatin
2	packages strawberries,		

Instructions

Mix crust ingredients together and spread in a 13 x 9" pan. Bake at 350 degrees for 10 minutes and cool.

Filling:
Combine the filling ingredients and spread over crust.

Topping:
Dissolve gelatin in boiling water. Drain juice from the strawberries and mix juice with gelatin. Add strawberries and allow to firm slightly before spreading over the filling.

TURNING THANKS

Fruit Salad

In Memory of Elise Caperton Boyett

Ingredients

- 1 can peach pie filling
- 1 small can maraschino cherries, drained and chopped
- ½ cup raisins, soaked, drained, and chopped
- 1 can pineapple tidbits, drained and chopped
- 2 bananas, chopped
- 2 tablespoons lemon juice (on top of bananas)
- ½ cup sugar
- 1 small can mandarin oranges

Instructions

Mix all the ingredients and serve. You can mix the night before, but do not add bananas until ready to serve.

SALADS

Mandarin Almond Salad
Ramona Robertson

Ingredients
for salad:

½	cup sliced almonds	1	small red onion, chopped
3	tablespoons sugar	1	11 oz. can mandarin oranges, drained
1	bunch red leaf lettuce, torn in bite-size pieces		

for dressing:

½	teaspoon salt	2	tablespoons sugar
¼	cup vegetable oil	2	tablespoons vinegar
1	tablespoon chopped parsley		dash of hot pepper sauce
			dash of pepper

Instructions

In a small skillet, heat the almonds and sugar on low. Cook and stir constantly until almonds are coated with a sugar glaze. Remove and allow to cool.

Combine all dressing ingredients and set aside.

Just before serving, toss lettuce, onion, and oranges with the dressing and almonds.

NOTES

NOTES

Fried Chicken is always a favorite with the kids!

ENTREES

TURNING THANKS

Poke and Eggs

In Memory of Tommye Haywood

"Everything that lives and moves about will be food for you. Just as I gave you the green plants, I now give you everything."

Genesis 9:3

Ingredients
- 2 pounds poke salad
- 6 eggs
- 6 tablespoons bacon drippings

Instructions
Parboil the poke salad in salt water until tender, drain well.

Place in a skillet with bacon drippings and simmer until all water is cooked out of the poke.

Scramble six eggs with the poke and add salt and pepper to taste.

Poke salad got its name from people picking the wild greens and placing them in a poke (paper sack) to take home.

ENTREES

Boiled Country Ham (Lard Stand)

Gail Pigg

Ingredients
1   cured ham up to 20 pounds
cold water as needed

Charles and Gail Pigg furnish the country ham for the church breakfasts.

Instructions
Place the ham in a lard stand, cover with cold water, and let soak overnight.

Pour old water off and cover with fresh cold water.

Place on high heat on stove, bring to a boil and boil for 1 hour.

Remove from heat, leaving the ham in the water.

Set on the floor on top of old magazines. Tie newspapers around the sides and top of the lard stand. Cover with blankets, quilts, or any type of heavy covering and leave for 24 hours.

Be careful when removing the ham as water will still be hot.

When the ham is cooled, trim off the excess fat and it is ready to slice.

This recipe is in the old Home Demonstration Cookbook and was submitted by Ms. Esther Cole, then the Home Demonstration Agent. This is the old fashioned way.

TURNING THANKS

Baked Ham

Kim Dickinson (recipe from mother-in-law, Jewell Dickinson)

Ingredients
1	large ham	½	cup brown sugar
1	can Coca-Cola		pineapple rings

Instructions
Place ham in a large roasting pan. Pour 1 can Coca-Cola over the ham and sprinkle with brown sugar. Place pineapple rings on top of ham. Cover and bake in 350 to 400 degree oven until done.

June 5, 1965: Shirley A. Walters and James R. Hanbac
The first wedding held in the remodeled church

ENTREES

Oven Baked Country Ham

Marie Vestal Walters

Ingredients
1   country ham   1   cup brown suger

Instructions
Wash the country ham. Let stand in clear water over night. Remove 4 to 6 inches of the hock end. Save hock end for use in boiling beans.

Before cooking, rub 1 cup of brown sugar on meat side of ham. Wrap in 2 layers of heavy duty aluminum foil. Place wrapped ham (skin side up) in a deep covered pan and fill pan with water. Bake in preheated oven 350 degrees for 4 hours.

After cooking time, turn off oven and leave overnight 8 to 12 hours. Remove from oven. Remove foil and drain excess drippings. Remove skin and let cool at room temperature.

Wrap and place in refrigerator for 24 hours to make slicing easy.

TURNING THANKS

Honey-Pecan Pork Cutlets

Jim Hanback

"So Elisha left him and went back. He took his yoke of oxen and slaughtered them. He burned the plowing equipment to cook the meat and gave it to the people, and they ate. Then he set out to follow Elijah and became his attendant."

1 Kings 19:21

Ingredients

- 4 pork cutlets, tenderized, ¼-inch thick
- 4 tablespoons flour
- ½ teaspoon salt
- ¼ teaspoon ground black pepper
- 1 tablespoon butter
- ¼ cup honey
- ¼ cup chopped pecans

Instructions

Season flour with salt and pepper; dust surfaces of pork with seasoned flour. Melt butter in large heavy skillet over medium-high heat.

Brown cutlets on one side, turn; stir together honey and pecans and add to skillet, stir gently. Cover and simmer for 7-8 minutes.

Serve cutlets with sauce from skillet.

ENTREES

Tender Pork Chops and Gravy

Marie Vestal Walters

Ingredients

6	pork chops	1	can mushroom soup
2	tablespoons cooking oil	1	soup can of water
	salt and pepper		

Instructions

Sprinkle pork chops with salt and pepper, then dredge each chop in flour. Heat oil in skillet and brown pork chops on both sides. Remove from skillet and place in a 9 x 13" baking dish.

Mix mushroom soup and water until well blended. Pour soup mixture over browned pork chops and cover dish with aluminum foil.

Place in oven that has been preheated to 350 degrees and bake for 1 to 1½ hours, depending on the thickness of the pork chops.

The chops will be tender enough to cut with a fork and the soup mixture makes delicious gravy.

Variation: instead of mushroom soup, cover chops with brown gravy (store bought or homemade).

Variation: Instead of pork chops, use round steak.

TURNING THANKS

Quick Sweet & Sour Pork

Marie Vestal Walters

Ingredients

- 2 tablespoons corn oil
- 1 lb. boneless pork, cut in 1-inch cubes
- 1 20 oz. can pineapple chunks
- ½ cup Karo white syrup
- ¼ cup cider vinegar
- 2 tablespoons ketchup
- 2 tablespoons soy sauce
- 1 clove garlic, crushed
- ½ cup green pepper, cut in 1-inch squares
- 2 tablespoons corn starch
- 2 tablespoons water

Instructions

Heat oil over medium heat. Add pork and brown. Stir in next 6 ingredients and bring to a boil. Reduce heat and simmer uncovered, stirring occasionally, until pork is tender.

Add green pepper. Mix cornstarch and water and add to the cooked mixture. Stirring constantly, bring to a boil for 1 minute or until thickened.

Serve over rice or noodles.

ENTREES

Speedy Stir Fry Beef

Jim Hanback

Ingredients

1	lb. beef tip steak, $1/8$ to $1/4$-inch thick	3	oz. package beef ramen noodles
1	tablespoon vegetable oil	2	cups frozen Oriental vegetable combination
$1/8$	teaspoon ground red pepper	2	cups boiling water
		2	teaspoons light soy sauce

Instructions

Cut beef crosswise into 1-inch strips. Mix oil with red pepper. Coat strips with mixture.

Break noodles into pieces and add to vegetables in boiling water. Reserve seasoning packet. Allow to return to boil, then reduce heat. Simmer, uncovered, for 3 minutes.

Drain, then add seasoning packet.

Stir-fry half of beef in a skillet over medium-high heat for approximately 60 seconds. Repeat for second half of beef. Add soy sauce and stir in the nodles and vegetables. Heat until hot.

TURNING THANKS

Rib Eye Roast & Oven Browned Vegetables

Jim Hanback

[23] "'Bring the fattened calf and kill it. Let's have a feast and celebrate. [24] For this son of mine was dead and is alive again; he was lost and is found.' So they began to celebrate."

Luke 15:23-24

Ingredients

4	lbs. beef rib eye roast, small end, trimmed	2	teaspoons dried rosemary
2	tablespoons vegetable oil	4	cloves garlic, crushed
3	medium baking potatoes, quartered	1	teaspoon dry mustard
2	large sweet potatoes, cut into eighths	2½	teaspoons salt
4	small onions, halved	1	teaspoon cracked black pepper
		12	oz. prepared brown gravy
		¼	cup currant jelly

Instructions

Heat oven to 350 degrees. Combine seasoning ingredients: rosemary, garlic, 1 teaspoon dry mustard, salt and pepper. Press half the seasoning evenly into surface of beef roast. Add oil to remaining seasoning; reserve. Place roast on a rack in shallow baking dish. Insert meat thermometer into thickest part, not touching bone or fat. Roast in 350-degree oven approximately 1¾ hours for medium rare, 2 hours for medium.

Combine vegetables and reserved seasoning; toss to coat. About 1¼ hours before serving, arrange vegetables around roast.

ENTREES

Remove roast when thermometer registers 135 degrees for medium rare, 150 degrees for medium. Tent with foil and let stand 15 minutes; internal temperature will rise. Cook vegetables 15 minutes longer or until tender, stirring once.

For sauce, mix mustard with 1 teaspoon water in small saucepan until smooth. Stir in gravy and jelly. Cook over medium heat 5 minutes or until smooth and bubbly, stirring occasionally. Carve roast into slices; serve with vegetables and sauce.

Makes 6 to 8 servings.

Easter, 1972

TURNING THANKS

Reece's Slow Cook Pot Roast

Reece Robertson

Ingredients

1	(4 to 5 lb.) chuck, rump, or round roast	1	teaspoon salt
6–8	potatoes, cut in chunks	¼	teaspoon ginger
6–8	carrots, cut in bite-size chunks	¼	teaspoon caraway seed
¼	cup oil	¼	teaspoon sesame seed
2	medium onions, sliced	1	teaspoon minced garlic
2	(8 oz.) cans tomato sauce	½	cup chopped celery
2	cups water	2	packages brown and/or mushroom gravy mix
¼	teaspoon pepper	½	cup tomato juice

Instructions

Brown roast on all sides in oil. Place in slow cook pot and add onion, tomato sauce, water, pepper, ginger, caraway seed, sesame seed, garlic, and celery. Simmer for 6 to 7 hours.

Add carrots, potatoes, and salt. Simmer for 30 minutes,

Remove meat; let cool and slice.

Add packages of gravy mix to juice in slow cook pot and stir. Add tomato juice and cook for 15 minutes.

Return meat to gravy and vegetables; heat and serve.

ENTREES

Beef Stroganoff

Jim Hanback

Ingredients

1	lb. beef top sirloin steak	2	teaspoons vegetable oil
1½	cup uncooked bow tie pasta	1–2	tablespoons all-purpose flour
½	lb. mushrooms, cut into ½-inch slices	¾	cup beef broth
		1	tablespoon sliced green onion
⅓	cup coarsely chopped onion	¼	cup light sour cream

Instructions

Follow package directions for cooking bow tie pasta. Trim steak and cut into ½-inch cubes.

Grease a nonstick skillet with vegetable oil cooking spray and heat over medium-high heat.

Add beef and stir-fry until done. Add seasoning. Remove beef from skillet and keep warm.

Cook mushrooms and onion in the same skillet until tender. Add flour and gradually stir in broth. Boil, then stir over heat for 2 minutes.

Transfer beef to skillet and heat. Pour stir-fry over bow tie pasta. Top with green onion and dollops of sour cream.

TURNING THANKS

Pepper Steak

Janis Rozelle

Ingredients
- 1–1½ lbs. beef round steak
- 1 can tomatoes
- 2 onions, chopped
- 2–3 stalks celery, sliced
- 2–3 green or colored peppers, sliced
- ½ lb. mushrooms, sliced

Instructions
Cut meat into thin strips & coat with seasoned flour. Brown meat well in hot oil, then add 1 cup water and the juice from the can of tomatoes. Add sliced onions. Simmer about 1-1½ hours.

Add the celery and simmer another ½ hour.

Add tomatoes, peppers & mushrooms. Simmer another ½ hour.

Season to taste. Thicken with flour if needed.

Serve over hot cooked yellow rice.

Janis Rozelle, a native of New Orleans, is the mother of member Paula Rozelle Hanback.

ENTREES

Braised Sirloin Tips over Rice

Dana Walters

Ingredients

2	tablespoons shortening	2	teaspoons garlic powder
2	lbs. sirloin tip steak, cubed	½	teaspoon onion salt
2	10½ oz. cans beef consommé	4	tablespoons corn starch
		½	cup water
2	tablespoons soy sauce	2	cups cooked white rice

Instructions

Melt shortening in large skillet, brown meat on all sides. Drain any liquid.

Stir in consommé, soy sauce, garlic powder, onion salt. Bring to boil. Reduce, cover and simmer for 1 hour.

Blend corn starch and water and stir gradually into meat mixture, stirring constantly until mixture thickens and boils. Add more corn starch mixture if needed.

Serve over hot cooked rice.

TURNING THANKS

Jim's Meatloaf

Jim Hanback

Ingredients

1	lb. lean ground beef or turkey	½	cup crumbled saltine crackers or instant oatmeal
2	large eggs		
¼	cup worchestershire sauce	½	teaspoon salt
¾	cup Ketchup	½	teaspoon ground black pepper

Instructions

Place the meat and all other ingredients in a large mixing bowl and mix until you have a blended mixture.

Coat the bottom of 2 to 3 quart baking dish with olive oil.

Place the mixture in the baking dish and form a loaf.

Drizzle additional ketchup over the top to suit your taste.

Bake at 350 degrees for 45 minutes. You can vary the time to suit your taste.

ENTREES

Thrifty Meatballs

Marie Vestal Walters

"So he got up and ate and drank. Strengthened by that food, he traveled forty days and forty nights until he reached Horeb, the mountain of God."

1 Kings 19:8

Ingredients

1	lb. ground beef	⅓	cup milk
2½	teaspoons onion salt	1	10.5 oz. can condensed tomato, celery, or mushroom soup
¼	cup uncooked rice		
¼	cup crushed cracker crumbs, firmly packed		

Instructions

Mix all ingrdients except the condensed soup until well blended. Shape into small balls.

Place 2 tablespoons of shortening in a skillet and melt. Add meatballs and brown, turning as needed to brown all sides. Add the can of condensed soup and a can of water. Cook about 1 hour, stirring occasionally. Remove meatballs to a heated platter and bring juice to a boil. Thicken as needed.

Serve the juice over the meatballs, sprinkle with grated parmesan cheese and chopped parsley flakes. Wonderful when served over hot cooked spaghetti.

TURNING THANKS

Easy Stuffed Peppers

Jim Hanback

Ingredients

1	lb. lean ground beef	1	teaspoon dried oregano leaves, divided
4	medium green, red or yellow bell peppers	½	teaspoon salt
¾	cup chopped onion	¼	teaspoon pepper
¼	cup uncooked rice	1	14.5 oz. can Italian-style stewed tomatoes, undrained
3	tablespoons catsup, divided		

Instructions

Cut tops off bell peppers and remove seeds and membrane.

Combine ground beef, onion, and rice. Add 2 tbsp. catsup, ½ tsp. oregano and season with salt and pepper. Mix thoroughly. Spoon meat mixture into bell peppers and place in a baking dish.

Combine remaining ingredients and pour over stuffed peppers. Cover baking dish with foil. Bake at 350 degrees for 90 minutes.

Variations: Four large zucchini or yellow squash may be substituted for the bell peppers.
(Reduce cooking time by about 15 minutes.)

ENTREES

Stuffed Tomatoes

Janis Rozelle

Ingredients

6–8 ripe tomatoes	salt and pepper to taste
1 lb. hamburger	fresh or dried parsley
1 onion, chopped	fresh or dried thyme
1 package seasoned stuffing mix	flavored breadcrumbs
	butter

Instructions

Cut tops off tomatoes. Scoop out pulp & reserve. Put shells in a baking pan with about ¼" of water.

Brown hamburger and onion and drain. Cut up tomato pulp and add to hamburger mixture along with seasonings. Simmer until tomato is all liquid. Remove from heat and stir in enough stuffing mix to absorb all liquid.

Spoon filling into shells. Top each with a small pat of butter and a sprinkle of breadcrumbs. Bake at 350 for 30–45 minutes.

This is a great way to use up that late summer bounty of tomatoes!

TURNING THANKS

Easy Lasagna

Shirley Hanback

Ingredients

6	lasagna noodles	16	oz. cottage cheese (small curd or creamed)
1	lb. ground beef		
1	jar spaghetti sauce (use whatever flavor you prefer)	1	8 oz. package shredded mozzarella cheese
		1	teaspoon oregano
		½	cup parmesan cheese

Instructions

Cook noodles in boiling salted water until tender, using package instructions. Remove from heat, drain and rinse in cold water to prevent noodles from sticking together while preparing the sauce.

Brown crumbled ground beef in a separate pan over medium heat. Drain off excess fat and add spaghetti sauce and oregano. Continue cooking until well blended, approximately 8–10 minutes.

In a 9 x 13" baking dish, layer 3 noodles and half of the cottage cheese, mozzarella cheese, and spaghetti sauce mixture. Repeat layers using the remaining ingredients in the same order, ending with sauce. Sprinkle the Parmesan cheese on top and bake at 375 degrees for about 30 minutes. Allow the dish to cool 10–15 minutes before serving.

ENTREES

Baked Hot Chicken Salad
Gina Dodson Griggs

"Then their father Israel said to them, 'If it must be, then do this: Put some of the best products of the land in your bags and take them down to the man as a gift—a little balm and a little honey, some spices and myrrh, some pistachio nuts and almonds.' "

Genesis 43:11

Ingredients
- 2 cups cubed or shredded chicken breasts
- 2 tablespoons fresh lemon juice
- ½ teaspoon salt
- ½ teaspoon pepper
- ½ cup slivered almonds
- 1 cup diced celery
- 1 cup mayonnaise
- 1 cup shredded cheddar cheese
- ⅔ cup crushed potato chips

Instructions
Mix all ingredients together and place in a lightly greased 13 x 9" baking dish. Add crushed potato chips to top and bake at 350 degrees for 20 minutes.

TURNING THANKS

Chicken Casserole 1

In Memory of Marie Hood

Ingredients

4	cups chicken, cooked and cut up	1	can condensed chicken soup
2	cups celery	1	cup mayonnaise
¼	cup onion		

for topping:
shredded cheese   potato chips, crushed

Instructions

Mix together all ingredients. Pour into baking dish and bake at 350 degrees until it begins to bubble.

Sprinkle cheese (cheddar or American) and crushed potato chips on top of the casserole and continue baking until slightly browned.

ENTREES

Chicken Casserole 2

Stella Jones

"They asked, and he brought them quail and satisfied them with the bread of heaven."

Psalm 105:40

Ingredients

3	large boneless chicken breasts	1½	cup cooked rice
1	package 8 oz. sour cream	1	package shredded cheese, 16 oz., your choice
1	can cream of chicken soup	1	sleeve Ritz crackers or 2 cups crushed Corn Flakes
1	can cream of mushroom soup		

Instructions

Boil chicken till well done, then shred into large pan. Boil rice till done. Then add rice, both cans of soup and sour cream to chicken and mix well. Sprinkle shredded cheese over top. Top with crushed crackers or Corn Flakes (your choice) and place in oven for 20 min at 400 degrees or until top is golden brown. Enjoy.

TURNING THANKS

Chicken Casserole 3

Joann Berry by Marie Vestal Walters

"Jerusalem, Jerusalem, you who kill the prophets and stone those sent to you, how often I have longed to gather your children together, as a hen gathers her chicks under her wings, and you were not willing."

Matthew 23:37

Ingredients

- 4 chicken breasts, cooked and sliced
- 1 cup Minute rice
- 1 cup celery, chopped
- 2 tablespoons onions, chopped
- 1 can cream of chicken soup
- ½ cup mayonnaise
- 1 cup Corn Flakes
- 2 tablespoons butter, melted
- salt and pepper to taste

Instructions

Assemble all ingredients through mayonnaise and mix. Cover with Corn Flakes. Pour melted butter over flakes.

Bake at 325 degrees for 45 minutes.

ENTREES

Chicken Casserole 4

Dana Walters

Ingredients

1	pack of Ritz crackers	1	can cream of chicken soup (Campbell's only)
1	stick butter		
3–4	chicken breasts, shredded	1	8 oz. sour cream
		1/8	cup milk

Instructions

Crumble up crackers in bowl. Melt butter and pour over crackers. (Use extra crackers if you don't like them too buttery.)

Mix chicken, sour cream, milk, cream of chicken soup together. Add extra milk if a creamier texture is desired.

Put ½ of crackers in bottom of dish, add mixture, and put remaining crackers on top.

Bake at 350 degrees for 35 minutes. You can make 1 day and bake the next.

Dana says: "double this recipe!"

TURNING THANKS

Chicken Enchiladas

Carrie Dhanarajan

"Take along these ten cheeses to the commander of their unit. See how your brothers are and bring back some assurance from them."

1 Samuel 17:18

Ingredients

4	boneless chicken breasts	1	large can enchilada sauce (whatever heat you prefer)
1	package enchilada seasoning	8	burrito size soft tortillas
½	medium size jar picante sauce	1	package shredded cheddar cheese
			sour cream as desired

Instructions

In a large skillet, heat enough olive oil to cover the bottom. Cook the chicken until done, cutting it up as it begins to brown. Once cooked thoroughly, add the enchilada mix and a little water. Stir well. Add desired amount of picante sauce to taste (about half of a medium-sized jar). Bring to a boil, then lower the heat and simmer about 10 minutes.

Pour some of the enchilada sauce in the bottom of a casserole dish. Place chicken mixture in the tortillas and add cheese. Roll and place in dish. Repeat with remaining tortillas. Pour the remaining enchilada sauce over the enchiladas and cover with cheese. Bake at 350 for about 30 minutes or until the cheese is melted and bubbly.

ENTREES

Lemon Garlic Chicken
Jim Hanback

Ingredients
4	boneless, skinless chicken breasts	¾	cup uncooked rice
1	tablespoon margarine or butter	2	chicken bouillon cubes
		1	lemon, halved
3	clove garlic, minced	1½	cup frozen broccoli, carrots and cauliflower
2	cup water		

Instructions
Grease a nonstick skillet with melted margarine. Cook chicken over medium-high heat for 5-7 minutes.

Add garlic to chicken and cook for 1 minute, then add water, rice, bouillon, and juice from half of lemon. Boil.

Once boiling, reduce heat and cover. Allow to simmer for 20 minutes.

Add remaining ingredients, reserving lemon halves, and cook for 5 minutes or until chicken is done.

When done, slice remaining lemon half and add as garnish.

TURNING THANKS

Turkey Divan

Shirley Hanback

Ingredients

4 lbs. cooked turkey or chicken or 6 whole chicken breasts	2 10 oz. packages of frozen broccoli, thawed

Sauce:
- 2 10¾ oz. cans cream of chicken soup
- 1 cup mayonnaise
- 1 teaspoon lemon juice
- ½ teaspoon curry powder
- ½ cup shredded sharp cheese

Topping:
- ½ cup toasted bread crumbs
- 1 tablespoon melted margarine

Instructions

In lightly greased 9 x 13" dish, layer the turkey and the broccoli. Prepare the sauce by mixing the ingredients and pour over the broccoli and turkey. Combine margarine and crumbs. Sprinkle over sauce. Bake at 350 degrees for 25-30 minutes.

Note: This recipe can be used with chicken or turkey. It can easily be cut in half for a smaller group.

> This is a great way to use leftover Thanksgiving or Christmas turkey.
> It can also be made ahead of time and then heated.

ENTREES

Garlic Salmon Fillet

Jim Hanback

Ingredients

½	teaspoon ground oregano	2	cup mushrooms, fresh, pieces or slices
¼	teaspoon black pepper		
4	teaspoons olive oil	4	cloves garlic, minced
2	medium oranges	½	cup green onions, chopped
2	teaspoons orange peel, raw		
1	cup carrots, strips or slices	4	salmon fillets, 3 oz. each

Instructions

Preheat oven to 350 degrees.

In a small saucepan, cook carrots, covered, in a small amount of boiling water for approximately 2 minutes. Drain and set aside. In a large bowl combine carrots, mushrooms, green onions, orange peel, oregano, garlic, and ¼ teaspoon pepper. Toss gently to combine.

Prepare four 18 x 12" pieces of heavy duty aluminum foil. Divide the vegetables evenly in the center of each piece of foil. Place a salmon fillet on top of each stack of vegetables. Drizzle 1 teaspoon of olive oil over each salmon. Sprinkle lightly with additional pepper and place orange slices on top.

Fold and seal the aluminum foil around each piece, allowing room for steam. Place foil packs on a baking tray in single layer and bake for 30 minutes or until carrots are done and fish is flaky.

TURNING THANKS

Baked Cod

Jim Hanback

"He said, Throw your net on the right side of the boat and you will find some. When they did, they were unable to haul the net in because of the large number of fish."

John 31:6

Ingredients
2	large eggs	4	fish fillets, cod or other
1	dash black pepper	2	slices wheat bread, or bread crumbs
1	teaspoon water		

Instructions

If using whole bread, use a food processor to process the bread into fine crumbs. Place crumbs in a small bowl.

Beat eggs and water together. Season the fish with pepper. Dip the fish into the egg mixture and then in the bread crumbs. Place fish on a sprayed baking sheet. Generously coat the breaded fish with cooking spray. Bake at 400 degrees for approximately 10 minutes or until fish is opaque.

ENTREES

Meal in One
Shirley Hanback

Ingredients
- 2½ cups uncooked macaroni
- 2 tablespoon oil
- 6 tablespoons chopped onion
- 2 lbs. ground beef
- 1 tablespoon salt
- 1 dash pepper
- 1-2 tablespoons chili powder if desired
- 1 cup grated American cheese
- 3 cups canned or cooked tomatoes

Instructions
Cook macaroni in a large amount of boiling salted water until tender. Drain and rinse in cold water. Brown onions in oil, add beef, salt, and pepper and cook until meat is browned. Add macaroni, tomatoes, and chili powder. Put into a baking dish and sprinkle cheese over top.

Bake at 400 degrees for 30 minutes or until cheese is melted.

Great served over fried cornbread.

TURNING THANKS

Mexican Meal in One (Casserole)

Jim Hanback

Ingredients

- 2 lbs. lean ground beef
- 1 envelope taco seasoning
- ¾ cup water
- 2 16 oz. cans refried beans
- 1 small jar salsa
- 6 flour tortillas (6" or larger)
- 1 can niblet corn, drained
- 4 cups mexican shredded chesse

Instructions

Cook beef until done, break up as fine as possible, drain fat. Add taco seasoning and water. Bring to a boil, reduce and simmer for 5 minutes.

Mix the refried beans and salsa together and heat in a microwave for 1–2 minutes or until spreadable.

Place 3 tortillas in the bottom of a greased 2 ½ quart baking dish. Spread half of the ground beef over them.

Place a layer of the beans and salsa over the meat, then a layer of niblet corn. Spread the shredded cheese over the corn.

Repeat the layering with tortillas, beef, beans, corn, and cheese. Bake at 350 degrees for 40–45 minutes or until cheese is melted.

Serve with lettuce, tomatoes, and sour cream on top if desired.

ENTREES

Farmer's Strata

Marie Vestal Walters

Ingredients

10	slices white bread, sour dough preferred	3	cups cheddar cheese
1	cup potatoes, cooked and cubed	8	eggs
		3	cups milk
1	lb. bacon, cut in 1-inch slices	1	tablespoon Worchestershire sauce
2	cups cooked ham	1	teaspoon dry mustard
1	small onion, chopped		salt and pepper to taste

Instructions

In a large skillet, cook bacon over medium heat until crisp; add ham and onion. Cook and stir until onion is tender; drain.

In a greased 13 x 9 x 2" baking dish, layer half of the bread cubes, potatoes, and cheese. Top with all of the bacon mixture. Repeat layers of bread, potatoes, and cheese.

In a bowl, beat the eggs; add milk, Worcestershire sauce, mustard, salt, and pepper. Pour over all. Cover and chill overnight.

Remove from refrigerator 30 minutes before baking. Bake, uncovered, at 325 degrees for 65–70 minutes or until a knife inserted near the center comes out clean.

TURNING THANKS

Veggie Pot Pie

Carrie Dhanarajan

"Better a meal of vegetables where there is love than a fattened calf with hatred."

Proverbs 15:17

Ingredients
for the filling:

3	stalks celery, chopped	2	cups vegetable broth
½	onion, chopped	1	cup plain soy milk
3	carrots, chopped	1	teaspoon salt
3	tablespoons Earth Balance vegan margarine	1	teaspoon pepper
		¾	cup frozen peas
½	cup flour	¾	cup frozen edamame

for the crust:

1	cup flour	⅓	cup Earth Balance margarine
1	teaspoon salt	2-3	tablespoons cold water

Instructions
Filling:
Saute celery, onions, and carrots in butter for 10 minutes.

Add the flour, stirring constantly for 1 minute. Add broth and milk to mixture while stirring constantly.

Cook over medium heat until bubbly, then stir in the peas, edamame, salt, and pepper.

ENTREES

Pour into a 2-quart casserole dish and top with crust.

Bake at 375 degrees for 30-45 minutes.

Crust:
Mix flour and salt together, cut in shortening, add the water, then shape into a ball and chill. Once it's chilled, roll out the dough to fit the casserole dish.

Pastor and Mrs. Usry at the 100th Anniversary of Akin Chapel

TURNING THANKS

Island Burger

James Hanback, Jr.

Ingredients
- 4 hamburger buns, regular
- 1 lb. ground beef
- 1 can pineapple rings (or fresh)
- 1 chopped green pepper
- ½ cup chopped onion
- 2 tablespoons ketchup
- 2 tablespoons A1 steak sauce

Instructions
If required, slice pineapple into hamburger bun-sized rings. Lightly char the pineapple slices on the grill for added flavor.

Knead ketchup and A1 steak sauce into ground beef. Shape ground beef into four ¼-lb. patties and fry or grill to taste.

Place cooked hamburgers on bun and top with pineapple, onion, and green pepper. If desired, add extra hamburger toppings, such as cheese, lettuce, tomato, pickle, and mustard. Serves four.

This is a fun, easy recipe for a backyard luau around the swimming pool.
For picky eaters, you can set the suggested toppings out in separate containers and let them "build their own" island burger.

ENTREES

Soupy Burger

Shirley Hanback

"Wine that gladdens human hearts, oil to make their faces shine, and bread that sustains their hearts."

Psalm 104:15

Ingredients

1	lb. ground beef	1	small onion, chopped
1	can mushroom soup	2	teaspoons margarine
2	teaspoons mustard		split, toasted hamburger buns
2	teaspoons tomato ketchup		

Instructions

Melt margarine and brown the onions. Mix in the ground beef and cook until done.

Pour in the soup, ketchup, and mustard. Cook until creamy.

Serve over split, toasted hamburger buns.

Also great poured over pasta or fried cornbread.

TURNING THANKS

Hamburber BBQ

Paula Rozelle Hanback

Ingredients
- 1 lb. ground beef
- 1 can tomato sauce
- ½ bottle molasses
- 1 tablespoon mustard
- 4 hamburger buns

Directions
Brown ground beef in large skillet. Drain.

Add remaining ingredients (except buns). Cover with screen to avoid splattering. Simmer on low heat until sauce is thickened.

Serve hamburger mixture on warm buns.

Paula says, "Don't skimp on the molasses!"

NOTES

Gail Rountree Pigg is at the far right.
The little one in front of Gail is Vicki Dodson.

NOTES

NOTES

SIDES

TURNING THANKS

Scalloped Oysters

Marie Vestal Walters

"Land that drinks in the rain often falling on it and that produces a crop useful to those for whom it is farmed receives the blessing of God."

Hebrews 6:7

Ingredients
1	can bull head oysters	1	stack saltine crackers
1	stick butter		sweet milk (as needed)
4	hard boiled eggs		salt and pepper to taste

Instructions
Layer oysters in a casserole dish. Cover with cracker crumbs.

Add layer of sliced hard boiled eggs.

Salt and pepper to taste.

Cover with cracker crumbs. Slice butter over crumbs and fill with milk.

Bake at 400 degrees for 20 minutes.

SIDES

Ronald Reagan's Favorite Mac and Cheese

Carrie Dhanarajan

Ingredients

- 2 cups macaroni
- 1 teaspoon butter
- ½ teaspoon salt
- 1 teaspoon dry mustard (can substitute prepared mustard)
- 3 cups grated sharp cheddar cheese
- 2 cups milk

Instructions

Boil macaroni until tender and drain well. Stir in butter and egg.

Mix salt and mustard with 1 tablespoon hot water and add to milk.

Add cheese to noodles, reserving enough to sprinkle on top. Pour noodles and cheese into buttered casserole dish, add milk.

Sprinkle with cheese.

Bake at 350 for 45 minutes or until custard is set and top is crusty.

TURNING THANKS

Pasta with Broccoli and Pine Nuts

Jim Hanback

"So I commend the enjoyment of life, because there is nothing better for a person under the sun than to eat and drink and be glad. Then joy will accompany them in their toil all the days of the life God has given them under the sun."

Ecclesiastes 8:15

Ingredients

- 8 oz. spinach pasta, or rainbow style
- 2 cups broccoli florets and stems
- 2 cloves garlic, peeled and minced
- 2 tablespoons pine nuts, pecans, almonds, or your preference
- 3 cups tomatoes, chopped
- 1 tablespoon olive oil
- salt to taste

Instructions

Cook pasta until tender, drain and set aside. Break broccoli into florets and dice stems.

Combine broccoli, ½ cup tomatoes, pine nuts, and garlic and steam for 5 to 10 minutes.

Remove from steam and stir in the rest of the tomatoes, olive oil, and seasonings.

You can serve over the pasta or mix in with the vegetables. For meat lovers, you can add chopped chicken, pork, or beef.

SIDES

Wild Rice Medley

Shirley Hanback

Ingredients

- 1½ tablespoons olive oil
- ½ cup celery, chopped
- ½ cup onion, chopped
- 2½ cups chicken broth
- 1 cup wild rice
- ½ cup pecans
- ½ cup dried cranberries
- 1½ teaspoon grated orange zest
- 3 tablespoons chopped fresh parsley

Instructions

Heat oil on medium. Sauté onion and celery for 5 minutes. Add broth and rice and bring to boil. Reduce to low heat and simmer 56-65 minutes or until rice is tender and liquid is absorbed.

Toast pecans at 325 degrees for 5–10 minutes. Mix pecans and cranberries into wild rice, then fold in orange zest and sprinkle with parsley.

TURNING THANKS

Cornbread & Sausage Stuffing

Bertha Lopez

Ingredients

- 3 cups cornbread cubes
- ½ cup pecan halves
- 6 oz. Italian sausage
- ½ cup celery, chopped
- 1 onion, chopped
- ½ green pepper, chopped
- 1 clove garlic, minced
- ¼ teaspoon Tony Chachere's creole seasoning
- ⅓ cup chicken broth
- 1 egg, beaten
- parsley

Instructions

Heat oven to 350. Toast cornbread on baking sheet until golden (15 mins). Add pecans after 10 minutes. Let pecans cool and break into pieces.

Cook sausage in a large skillet until browned. Set aside sausage and discard all but 2 tablespoons fat. Sauté onion, celery, green pepper, and garlic until tender. Add seasoning.

Combine cornbread, pecans, sausage, and sautéed vegetables in large bowl. Slowly add broth & egg, tossing gently until just moist. Spoon into large buttered baking dish. Bake uncovered for 35 minutes or until top is browned.

This recipe is easily doubled for a holiday meal (or lunch on the ground!)

SIDES

Corn Casserole

Norma Jones

"At mealtime Boaz said to her, Come over here. Have some bread and dip it in the wine vinegar. When she sat down with the harvesters, he offered her some roasted grain. She ate all she wanted and had some left over."

Ruth 2:14

Ingredients

- ½ cup corn meal
- 1 tablespoon flour
- 1 14.75 oz. can whole kernel corn, undrained
- 1 can cream style corn
- 1 egg
- 1 cup sour cream
- ½ stick butter

Instructions

Melt the butter in a casserole dish.

Mix all other ingredients together and pour over the butter.

Bake at 350 degrees for 30–35 minutes or until golden brown on top.

TURNING THANKS

Mixed Vegetable Casserole

Sarah Williams

"Do you not know that your bodies are temples of the Holy Spirit, who is in you, whom you have received from God? You are not your own."

1 Corinthians 6:19

Ingredients

- 2 cans Veg-all mixed vegetables
- 1 cup mayonnaise
- 1 small onion, chopped
- 1 cup chopped celery
- 1½ cup grated American cheese
- 1 stick margarine, melted
- 1 stack Ritz crackers, crushed

Instructions

Place vegetables in a greased casserole dish.

Mix mayonnaise, chopped onion, chopped celery, and grated cheese and spread over the vegetables.

Mix the cracker crumbs with melted margarine and sprinkle on top.

Bake 30 minutes at 350 degrees.

SIDES

Green Bean Casserole

Tammy Walters

Ingredients

- 2 cans French style green beans, drained
- 2 cans mushroom soup
- 1 large onion, diced finely
- 1 cup grated sharp cheese
- 1 can water chestnuts, sliced
- 1 can French fried onion rings
- 1 package slivered almonds

Instructions

Layer ingredients in a baking dish as follows: beans, soup, onion, cheese, chestnuts, and ½ of the almonds.

Bake at 350 degrees for 1 hour. Sprinkle with French onion rings and remaining almonds and cook for 5 minutes longer.

TURNING THANKS

Green Beans

Kim Dickinson (recipe from mother-in-law, Jewell Dickinson)

Ingredients
- green beans (fresh or canned)
- ¼ cup oil
- ½ cup onions, chopped
- ½ can Mountain Dew

Instructions
Put green beans in a large pot. Add oil and onions. Let this cook down a good bit until no water is left in the pot. Add ½ can of Mt. Dew and cook down again. Serve.

Easter, 2011

SIDES

Cowboy Baked Beans

Dana Walters

Ingredients
- 1 lb. ground beef, browned
- ½ onion, chopped
- ½ bell pepper, chopped
- 1 extra-large can baked beans or pork & beans plus 1 (16 oz.) size can
- ½ cup brown sugar
- ¼ cup pancake syrup (more or less to your taste)
- 1–2 tablespoons mustard
- 2–3 tablespoons catsup

Instructions
Mix all ingredients and pour into 9 x 13" Pyrex dish. Bake at 400 degrees for 1 hour.

TURNING THANKS

Potato Salad — Old Fashioned

Marie Vestal Walters

"For those who eat and drink without discerning the body of Christ eat and drink judgment on themselves."

1 Corinthians 11:29

Ingredients

4	medium potatoes, boiled, diced	¼-½	cup sweet pickle relish
1	onion, large, diced		salt to taste
4	eggs, hard boiled, diced	1	cup salad dressing

Instructions

Boil potatoes until tender, cool and dice. Dice the onion and hard boiled eggs.

Mix together and add the salad dressing.

SIDES

Potato Pancakes
Paula Rozelle Hanback

Ingredients
4	large russet potatoes, peeled	3	tablespoons all-purpose flour
1	small white onion, finely grated	1	tablespoon coarse salt
2	large eggs, lightly beaten	1	tsp. nutmeg
			salt and pepper to taste
			vegetable oil, for frying

Instructions
Grate the potatoes onto several layers of paper towels or a clean kitchen towel. When all are grated, squeeze out the excess water from the gratings, and place then in a large bowl.

Add onions, eggs, flour, nutmeg, salt, and pepper and stir well.

Heat vegetable oil in a large non-stick skillet. Spoon potato mixture into hot oil, using about ¼ cup of mixture for each pancake. Fry until golden brown, 4 to 6 minutes. Serve with applesauce.

TURNING THANKS

BLT Potatoes

Reece Robertson

Ingredients
- 4 potatoes, sliced
- 4 slices bacon, cooked crisp and crumbled
- ½ cup onion, chopped and sautéed
- ½ cup tomatoes, chopped
- ¾ cup chicken broth

Instructions
Cook potatoes, with salt and pepper added, in enough water to cover (do not overcook). Drain and add remaining ingredients. Cook another 15 minutes and serve.

SIDES

Parmesan Potatoes

Shirley Hanback

Ingredients

6	large potatoes	⅛	teaspoon pepper
¼	cup sifted flour	⅓	cup butter or oleo
¼	cup Parmesan cheese		chopped parsley
¾	teaspoon salt		

Instructions

Peel potatoes and cut into quarters. Place potatoes, along with next 4 ingredients, into a plastic bag that you can shake. Add water to bag and shake until potatoes are coated.

Coat a 9 x 13" baking pan with melted butter and layer potatoes in the pan.

Bake for 60 minutes at 375 degrees. At 30 minutes, turn potatoes.

Sprinkle with parsley.

Variation:

You can add 4 whole chicken legs or breasts to this recipe for a one-dish meal. Just shake the chicken in the same coating and bake all in one pan.

TURNING THANKS

Hash Brown Casserole

Chrystal Cole

Ingredients
1	bag of shredded frozen hash brown potatoes	1	medium sweet onion, chopped
1	can cream chicken soup	1	stick butter, melted
1	8 oz. container sour cream		Lowry's seasoned salt to taste

Instructions
Mix all ingredients together. Put in microwave safe glass bowl or dish. Microwave for 40 minutes.

the old Alexander Methodist Church that Akin Church bought for $500.

SIDES

Ratatouille

Jim Hanback

"He makes grass grow for the cattle, and plants for people to cultivate bringing forth food from the earth"

Psalm 104:14

Ingredients

2	tablespoons olive oil	1½	cup canned tomatoes or 2 chopped tomatoes
2	medium onions		
4	cloves garlic, crushed	1	teaspoon dried basil
3	red, yellow, or orange bell peppers	½	teaspoon dried oregano
		1	tablespoon dried parsley
1	medium eggplant	½	teaspoon salt
2	medium zucchini		

Instructions

Cut all vegetables into large chunks. Sauté onion in oil for 2 minutes.

Add garlic and remaining vegetables and sauté for a few minutes more. Add tomatoes and herbs and simmer covered for 15–20 minutes. Serve with brown rice.

TURNING THANKS

Squash Casserole

Frances Haywood Woodall Fraser

Ingredients

2	cups squash, cooked and mashed	½	cup mayonnaise
1	egg, well beaten	½	teaspoon salt
⅓	cup onion, chopped	3	tablespoons sugar
½	stick butter	½	cup cheese, grated
½	cup milk	1	as needed Ritz crackers, crushed

Instructions

Sauté onion in ¼ stick of butter. Mix with squash, egg, salt, and sugar.

Blend milk with mayonnaise and grated cheese. Mix into squash, blending well.

Pour into a 9 x 9" baking dish and top with crushed crackers.

Dot with remaining butter and bake for 25 minutes in a 350 degree oven.

SIDES

Stuffed Mushrooms
Shirley Hanback

Ingredients
4	slices bacon, diced	1	3 oz. package cream cheese
¼	cup minced onions		
2	tablespoons green pepper, minced	1	lb. fresh mushrooms
		½	cup soft bread crumbs
½	teaspoon salt	1	tablespoon butter
½	teaspoon Worchestershire		

Instructions
Cook bacon, onion, and green pepper in a skillet. Remove from fat and mix in salt, Worchestershire sauce, and cream cheese.

Wash and dry mushrooms. Remove stems. Chop ½ cup of stems and mix with bacon mixture. Stuff mushrooms with the mixture. Top with bread crumbs. Put in a baking dish with ¼ cup of water. Bake 4 minutes at 350 degrees or 2 minutes in a microwave.

TURNING THANKS

Sweet Potato Bake
Audrey Hood

"This service that you perform is not only supplying the needs of the Lord's people but is also overflowing in many expressions of thanks to God."

2 Corinthians 9:12

Ingredients

2	1 lb. cans of sweet potatoes, drained	2	cups orange juice
1	cup brown sugar, packed	½	cup raisins
2	tablespoons cornstarch	¼	cup walnuts, chopped
½	teaspoon salt	1	teaspoon grated orange rind

Instructions

Stir together orange juice and raisins. Cook over high heat until mixture comes to a boil. Add remaining ingredients, mix well and pour over the potatoes. Bake uncovered for 30-40 minutes or until potatoes are tender.

SIDES

Sweet Potatoes

Marie Vestal Walters

Ingredients

2	cups sweet potatoes (cooked or canned)	¾	stick butter or margarine
1	cup sugar	½	teaspoon nutmeg
½	teaspoon cinnamon	2	whole eggs
1	cup sweet milk	1	cup raisins (optional)

for the topping:

1	cup coconut	1	cup pecans
1	cup brown sugar	⅓	cup flour
⅓	cup butter or margarine		

Instructions

Mash cooked sweet potatoes until creamy. Add eggs and milk and blend thoroughly. Stir in raisins. Pour mixture into a 9 x 13 x 2" greased casserole dish. Bake at 400 degrees for 20 minutes. Remove from oven and add topping.

Topping:

Blend ingredients together, adding margarine last. Spread topping on potatoes and bake at 375 degrees for 25 minutes longer.

TURNING THANKS

Sweet Milk Gravy

Marie Vestal Walters

Ingredients
- 2 tablespoons bacon drippings or use drippings from frying sausage
- 2 tablespoons flour
- 1½ cups sweet milk

Instructions
Heat drippings in skillet. Add flour to hot drippings and let it brown a little bit. Salt and pepper to taste. Add sweet milk and cook, stirring constantly until thickened.

This is so good over hot biscuits for breakfast, served with sliced tomatoes.

NOTES

Rev. & Mrs. E. P. Boyett, pictured above will complete their pastoral ministry on the Tennessee District at the 61st District Assembly in August. For the past 30 years they have served the largest circuit of churches in our denomination — Mt. Wesley, Hilltown, Akin Chapel, and Fly. A special Homecoming Day is planned in their honor July 29th.

NOTES

NOTES

You can tell this is a Southern cookbook —
Desserts is the longest section!

DESSERTS

TURNING THANKS

Carrot Cake 1

Grace McGowan by Janie Fox

Ingredients

for the cake:

1¾	cups sugar	2	teaspoons baking soda
1¼	cups oil	2	teaspoons cinnamon
4	egg whites	1	teaspoon baking powder
2	cups flour	3	cups carrots, grated
1	teaspoon salt	½	cup nuts (your choice)

for the filling:

1	can crushed pineapple, large	½	stick butter
		2	teaspoons vanilla
1	8 oz. package cream cheese	1	box powdered sugar

Instructions

Mix all the cake ingredients and bake at 350 degrees for 25–30 minutes. Cool completely.

Mix the powdered sugar, cream cheese, butter, and vanilla together for the filling. Spread the crushed pineapple and filling between the layers.

DESSERTS

Carrot Cake 2

In Memory of Frances Davis

Ingredients
for the cake:

2	cups sugar	1	teaspoon salt
1½	cups Wesson oil	2	teaspoons cinnamon
4	eggs, beaten	3	cups grated raw carrots
2	cups flour	½	cup chopped nuts
2	teaspoons baking powder	1	can crushed pineapple
2	teaspoons soda		

for the frosting:

1	8 oz. cream cheese (softened)	1	box powdered sugar
½	stick margarine or butter, softened	2	teaspoons vanilla

Instructions

Put sugar in mixing bowl, add 1 egg at a time (beat in cup). Add oil. Sift all dry ingredients. Add carrots and nuts. Fold into sugar mixture.

Bake in 3 cake pans lined with wax paper at 300 degrees. Cool.

Put pineapple between layers. Frost with cream cheese frosting.

Cream Cheese Frosting:
Beat cream cheese and butter together. Add powdered sugar and vanilla. Beat until smooth.

TURNING THANKS

Coconut Cake

Joann Caperton Berry

Ingredients

for the cake:

- 3 cups cake flour
- ¼ teaspoon salt
- 1 lb. confectioners sugar
- 1 cup sweet milk
- 2 teaspoons baking soda
- 1 cup butter or 2 sticks of margarine
- 4 eggs, separated
- 1 cup coconut

for the icing:

- 2½ cups sugar
- ½ cup corn syrup
- ½ cup water
- 2 egg whites
- ⅛ teaspoon salt
- 1 teaspoon vanilla
- 1 cup coconut

Instructions

Grease 2 round 9" cake pans with butter. Dust each pan with flour, tapping out excess; set aside.

Cream butter and sugar. Add beaten egg yolks. Sift together flour, salt, and baking powder. Beat in flour, milk, and coconut, alternating between wet and dry ingredients.

Using clean dry beaters, beat egg whites with pinch of salt in another large bowl until stiff but not dry. Fold beaten egg whites into batter.

DESSERTS

Divide batter between prepared pans and bake until toothpick inserted in center comes out clean, about 30–40 minutes.

Icing:
Bring corn syrup and salt just to a boil in a small pot over medium-high heat. Meanwhile, beat egg whites in a mixing bowl with an electric mixer on medium speed until soft peaks form, 2–3 minutes. Increase speed to high and gradually add corn syrup while beating constantly until stiff, glossy peaks form, 2–3 minutes. Fold in vanilla.

Put 1 of the cake rounds on a cake plate, spread one-third of the frosting on top, and sprinkle with ¼ cup of the coconut. Set the remaining cake round on top, then ice cake with the remaining frosting. Sprinkle top and sides with remaining coconut.

Joann and Jimmy Berry have four children: Jeff, Jeanie, Jill and Julie. Jill Berry Harris designed and fabricated our stained glass windows. Joann is the daughter of Frank Caperton, Sr. and Elise.

TURNING THANKS

Easy Coconut Cake

Marie Vestal Walters

Ingredients

1	box white cake mix	2	cups sugar
2	cups sour cream	2	9 oz. packages frozen coconut
1½	cup Cool Whip, thawed		

Instructions

Bake cake in 2 layers, following box directions. Let cool. Slice layers in half.

Combine sugar, sour cream, and coconut. Reserve 1 cup of mixture for frosting. Spread remainder between layers and on top.

Combine reserved cup of sour cream mixture with Cool Whip. Spread on top and sides of cake. Store in refrigerator for 2 days before slicing.

DESSERTS

Dark Chocolate Cake

Noma Jean Dodson

Ingredients
1	package devil's food cake mix	¼	cup vegetable oil
4	large eggs	1	package chocolate instant pudding and pie filling
1	cup sour cream	¾	cup chocolate chips (optional)
¾	cup water		

Instructions
Combine all ingredients except chocolate chips. Beat with mixer, then stir in chocolate chips.

Pour into a well-greased bundt pan and bake 50–60 minutes in a 350 degree preheated oven.

TURNING THANKS

Dirt Cake

Ashley Kelley

Ingredients
1   bag Oreo cookies
1   box cream cheese
1   box vanilla pudding
1   container Cool Whip
a little sour cream

Instructions
Mix the last 4 ingredients and add a few crumbled cookies to the mix. Crumble the rest of the cookies on top.

Ashley is a dedicated, active member of the congregation. She was only 7 years old at the writing of this cook book and eager to make her contribution to it.

DESSERTS

Variation

from Shirley Hanback

Ingredients

1¼	lb. Oreo cookies, blended till fine		cheese, softened
½	lb. melted margarine or butter	1	cup Powdered sugar
		1	large package instant vanilla pudding mix
1	12 oz. container Cool Whip	2	cups milk
		1	teaspoon vanilla
1	8 oz. package cream		

Instructions

Combine pudding and milk, blend until thick.
Combine margarine, Cool Whip, cream cheese, powdered sugar and vanilla.

In a large bowl or plastic flower pot layer as follows:
- Small amount of blended cookie crumbs
- Layer of pudding (about half)
- Layer of cookie crumbs
- Layer of Cool Whip mixture

Repeat layers, ending with cookie crumbs on top. Refrigerate for 24 hours. Decorate with plastic flower and serve with a garden trowel.

TURNING THANKS

Fresh Apple Cake

Shirley Hanback

"When the woman saw that the fruit of the tree was good for food and pleasing to the eye, and also desirable for gaining wisdom, she took some and ate it. She also gave some to her husband, who was with her, and he ate it."

Genesis 3:6

Ingredients

for the cake:

2	cups sugar	3	cups sifted flour
3	eggs	1	teaspoon salt
½	cup vegetable oil	1	teaspoon soda
1	teaspoon vanilla	3	cups fresh apples, grated

for the icing:

1	cup brown sugar	1	stick margarine or butter
¼	cup milk		

Instructions

Mix sugar, eggs, vegetable oil, and vanilla, then add flour, salt, soda, and apples.

Bake in a greased tube pan at 350 degrees for 1 hour. Five minutes before cooking time is done, fork the cake and pour the icing mixture on top. Finish baking. Let cool before removing from the pan.

Icing:
Mix the brown sugar, milk and butter and boil 3 minutes.

DESSERTS

Fruit Cocktail Cake

Marilyn Peach

Ingredients
for the cake:

2	cups sugar	2½	cups fruit cocktail
2¾	cups flour, self rising	1	cup nuts

for the icing:

1	stick butter	1	cup coconut
1½	cups sugar	1	cup nuts (walnuts)
1	cup Pet milk	1	teaspoon vanilla

Instructions
Mix all ingredients well, pour into greased pan. Cook at 350 degrees for 30 minutes.

Icing:
Bring to boil the butter, sugar, and Pet milk. Cook for 7 minutes. Add coconut, nuts, and vanilla.

Mix and spread over cake.

TURNING THANKS

Gooey Butter Cake

Gina Dodson Griggs

"Do not forget to show hospitality to strangers, for by so doing some people have shown hospitality to angels without knowing it."

Hebrews 13:2

Ingredients

for the cake:

1	18¼ oz. package yellow cake mix	1	egg
		8	tablespoons butter, melted

for the filling:

1	8 oz. package cream cheese, softened	1	teaspoon vanilla
		8	tablespoons butter, melted
2	eggs	1	16 oz. box powdered sugar

Instructions

Combine the cake mix, egg, and butter. Mix well with electric mixer. Pat the mixture into the bottom of a lightly greased 13 x 9" baking pan.

Filling:

In a large bowl, beat cream cheese until smooth. Add eggs, vanilla, and butter and mix well. Add powdered sugar and mix well. Spread over the cake batter.

Bake for 40–50 minutes at 350 degrees. Do not over bake. The center should be gooey.

DESSERTS

Hawaiian Orange Cake

Marie Vestal Walters

Ingredients
for the cake:

1	box orange supreme cake mix	1	3 oz. package instant vanilla pudding (use dry mix)
4	eggs		
½	cup oil	1	3 oz. package orange Jell-O (use dry mix)
1½	cups milk		

for the filling:

1	15 oz. can crushed pineapple, well drained	12	oz. frozen coconut
2	cups sugar	1	8 oz. container Cool Whip
8	oz. container sour cream		

Instructions
Preheat oven to 350 degrees.

Mix all ingredients in order listed. Pour into 2 greased and floured 9-inch cake pans and bake for approximately 30 minutes. Remove from oven and let cool on wire rack. Split each layer horizontally, making 4 layers.

Prepare filling and reserve 1 cup.

Stack layers, spreading filling between each layer.

Mix the saved cup of filling with Cool Whip and spread on top and sides of cake.

TURNING THANKS

Honey Bun Cake

Carol Walters

"She gets up while it is still night; she provides food for her family and portions for her female servants."

Proverbs 31:15

Ingredients

for the cake:

1	box yellow cake mix	¾	cup oil
8	oz. sour cream	½	cup sugar
4	eggs	¾	cup brown sugar

for the Cinnamon Mix:

¾	cup brown sugar	3	teaspoons cinnamon

for the frosting:

2	cups powdered sugar	1	teaspoon vanilla
3–4	tablespoons milk		

Instructions

Blend cake mix, sour cream, eggs, oil, and sugar. Pour ½ of batter into a greased 9 x 13" baking dish. Sprinkle ½ of cinnamon mix on top of batter. Repeat layers using the remainder of the batter and top with remaining cinnamon mix.

Bake at 300 degrees for 50 minutes. Mix frosting and pour over hot cake immediately upon removing from the oven.

Cool and cut in squares.

DESSERTS

Jam Cake

In Memory of Jessie Mae Lockhart

Ingredients

1	cup butter	1	teaspoon nutmeg
2	cups sugar	1	teaspoon cloves
1	cup buttermilk	1	teaspoon cinnamon
1	teaspoon soda	1	cup blackberry jam
4	eggs	1	cup raisins
3	cups flour	1	cup nuts, chopped

Instructions

Cream butter and eggs, adding one egg at a time, beating well after each egg.

Add soda, sugar, and soda and stir until it foams.

Add jam, nuts, and raisins.

Sift the flour and spices, add gradually to the batter beating well as you go.

Bake at 300 degrees until done. Ice with caramel icing.

Makes three layers.

Jesse Mae (Chitter, as she was called) was a long-time member of the church and was like an aunt to everyone.

TURNING THANKS

Orange Blossom Special Cake

Norma Younger Jones

Ingredients

for the cake:
- 1 box yellow cake mix
- 4 eggs
- ½ cup oil
- 1 can mandarin oranges with syrup

for the frosting:
- 1 large can crushed pineapple with juice
- 1 large container Cool Whip
- 1 package vanilla instant pudding
- 1 teaspoon vanilla

Instructions

Combine cake mix, eggs, oil, and mandarin oranges.

Bake in a sheet cake pan at 275 degrees for 45 to 50 minutes.

Frosting:
Mix crushed pineapple, Cool Whip, instant pudding and vanilla.

Chill in the refrigerator before serving.

Norma is the granddaughter of John Howard Younger, one of the founders of Mt. Wesley.

DESSERTS

Pineapple Cake

Stella Jones

"[26] Look at the birds of the air; they do not sow or reap or store away in barns, and yet your heavenly Father feeds them. Are you not much more valuable than they? [27] Who of you by worrying can add a single hour to his life?"

Matthew 6;26-27

Ingredients
1	box yellow cake mix	½	cup brown sugar
2	cans crushed pineapple		

Instructions
Bake cake according to directions.

Drain pineapple juice and reserve.

Mix pineapple and brown sugar in small bowl.

When cake is done, while still warm take a knife and poke holes in cake and pour juice over top. Then spread pineapple mixture over top.

TURNING THANKS

Skillet Cake

Ray Gibson

Ingredients

1	cup sugar	½	cup milk
1	cup self-rising flour	2	eggs
½	cup oil	1	teaspoon vanilla

Instructions

Mix sugar, oil, and eggs until creamy. Stir in flour and milk, then add vanilla. Pour into well-greased iron skillet and bake at 350 degrees until done.

This is a very old recipe. It's quick and easy and delicious. Makes a great base for strawberry shortcake --Just cover a slice of this cake with fresh strawberries and whipped cream.

DESSERTS

Srawberry Sheet Cake

Kimberly Kelley

"Who satisfies your desires with good things so that your youth is renewed like the eagle's."

Psalm 103:5

Ingredients

for cake:

2	cups self-rising flour	¼	cup mashed sweetened strawberries
2	cups sugar		
4	eggs	1	box strawberry Jell-O, dry mix
1	cup canola oil		
1	cup milk		

for icing:

½	stick softened magarine	¼	cup mashed sweetened strawberries
3–4	cups powdered sugar		

Instructions

Mix all cake ingredients and pour into a 9 x 13" greased baking pan. Bake at 350 degrees for 25–30 minutes or until a toothpick inserted in center comes out clean.

Icing:

Mix all ingredients until smooth. Add more powdered sugar and/or strawberries as needed for a spreading consistency. Mix well before adding extra sugar and strawberries.

Store in the refrigerator.

TURNING THANKS

Vanilla Wafer Cake

Elizabeth "Liz" Brunson

Ingredients

- 2 sticks butter
- 6 whole eggs
- 2 cups sugar
- 1 cup coconut
- 1 cup pecans
- 1 15 oz. box vanilla wafers (crushed)
- ½ cup milk

Instructions

Cream sugar and butter. Add eggs, milk, and vanilla wafers. Add coconut and pecans. Bake in tube pan for 2 hours at 275 degrees. Cool for 10 minutes in the pan, then remove.

For Icing:
Bring to boil 1 cup sugar and 1 cup orange juice. Pour over warm cake.

Variation: Bake at 350 degrees for 1½ hours.

DESSERTS

Pumpkin Roll

Agnes Williams

Ingredients

- 3 eggs, slightly beaten
- 1 cup sugar
- ¾ cup all-purpose flour
- ⅔ cup canned pumpkin
- ½ teaspoon cinnamon
- 1 teaspoon baking soda
- 2 cups powdered sugar, divided in half
- 2 tablespoons margarine
- ¾ teaspoon vanilla
- 1 8 oz. package cream cheese at room temperature
- 1 cup nuts, finely chopped

Instructions

Preheat oven to 375 degrees. Line a 10 x 15" jelly roll pan with wax paper. Grease or spray with cooking spray.

Combine eggs, sugar, flour, pumpkin, cinnamon, and baking soda. Pour batter into prepared pan and bake 15 minutes.

Immediately turn onto a clean towel (not terrycloth) dusted with 1 cup powdered sugar. Starting at narrow end, roll towel, wax paper, and hot cake together. Cool 20 minutes, unroll and remove wax paper.

Mix remaining sugar with margarine, vanilla, and cream cheese until smooth. Spread filling on cake. Sprinkle with nuts.

Re-roll and refrigerate. Cut when cold.

TURNING THANKS

Quick Fruit Cobbler

Noma Jean Dodson

Ingredients
¾ cup self-rising flour
1 cup sugar
½ cup sweet milk
½ stick melted butter or margarine
fruit

Instructions
Melt butter or margarine in dish. Mix flour, sugar, and milk together. Pour in dish with butter or margarine. Pour fruit on top. Bake in 450-degree oven for about 30 minutes.

DESSERTS

Peach Cobbler
Tina Baxter

Ingredients
1	can of peaches	1	cup sugar
1	stick butter	¾	cup milk
1	cup flour	1	teaspoon corn syrup

Instructions
Mix flour, sugar, and milk with corn syrup.

Melt butter in baking dish.

Pour flour mixture over butter, then add peaches.

Bake for 30 to 40 minutes till done.

TURNING THANKS

Blueberry Dump Cake

Jerry Walters

"So whether you eat or drink or whatever you do, do it all for the glory of God."

1 Corinthians 10:31

Ingredients

4	cups frozen blueberries	1	box yellow cake mix
½	cup sugar	1½	sticks butter

Instructions

Dump blueberries and sugar into a baking dish, stir together.

Sprinkle cake mix over the fruit.

Slice butter and spread on top.

Bake at 350 degrees for 45 to 60 minutes.

Serve with Cool Whip or ice cream.

DESSERTS

Pie Pastry

Noma Jean Dodson

Ingredients

2	cups plain flour	1	egg
1	teaspoon salt	1	teaspoon vinegar
1	teaspoon sugar		ice water (about 3½ tablespoons)
1	stick cold margarine, cut up		

Instructions

In blender, cut in flour, salt, sugar, and margarine.

Add egg, vinegar, and ice water. Blend till it forms a ball.

Roll out on floured surface. Makes 2 pie crusts.

TURNING THANKS

Old-Fashioned Chess Pie

In Memory of Frances Davis

Ingredients

- 3 whole eggs
- 3 tablespoons cocoa
- 1 cup sugar
- 1 large can Carnation milk
- 1 tablespoon flour
- 3 tablespoons melted butter

Instructions

Mix and cook in unbaked pie shell, slow.

The directions on some of these older recipes don't give a lot of detail! I guess back in the day everyone knew how to make a chess pie...

DESSERTS

Chocolate Chess Pie

Noma Jean Dodson

Ingredients

1½	cups sugar	1	teaspoon vanilla
3	tablespoons cocoa	1	small can evaporated milk
½	stick margarine	1	unbaked pie shell
2	eggs		

Instructions

Mix sugar and cocoa in bowl. Add margarine, eggs, and vanilla. Add milk. Stir until mixed.

Pour in pie shell and bake at 350 degrees till done.

TURNING THANKS

Chess Pie

Robbie Fox — Great Grandmother's Recipe

"Is tasteless food eaten without salt, or is there flavor in the white of an egg?"

Job 6:6

Ingredients

1¼	cups sugar	1	teaspoon vinegar
3	eggs	1	tablespoon cornmeal
¼	teaspoon vanilla	1	stick butter

Instructions

Combine all ingredients. Stir only enough to mix thoroughly. Do not beat. Pour into unbaked pie shell.

Bake at 325 degrees for 1 hour.

DESSERTS

Pecan Pie

Tammy Walters

Ingredients

3	eggs, beaten	¼	teaspoon salt
1	cup sugar	1½	teaspoons vanilla
1	cup dark corn syrup (Karo)	1	cup whole pecans
1	tablespoon butter, melted	1	9" unbaked pie shell (deep dish)

Instructions

Mix sugar, corn syrup, butter, salt, eggs, and vanilla. Fold in nuts.

Pour into chilled, unbaked pie shell and bake at 350 degrees for 50 minutes to 1 hour. Cool before serving.

TURNING THANKS

Apple Crunch Pie

Noma Jean Dodson

Ingredients

7 cups apples, peeled and sliced	3 tablespoons sugar
1 teaspoon lemon juice	4½ teaspoons ground cinnamon
1 teaspoon vanilla	1 tablespoon corn starch
⅓ cup brown sugar	3 tablespoons melted butter

for the streusel topping:

¾ cup all-purpose flour	6 tablespoons cold butter, cut up
¼ cup sugar	½ cup chopped walnuts

Instructions

In a large bowl, toss apples with lemon juice and vanilla. Combine sugars, cinnamon, and corn starch. Add to apples and toss to coat. Put in unbaked pie shell. Shell will be full.

Streusel Topping:

Combine flour and sugar. Cut in butter. Sprinkle over apples. Top with walnuts. Bake at 350 degrees for 55 to 65 minutes. Good with caramel drizzled over top.

DESSERTS

Banana Split Pie

Norma Jean Dodson

"He asked for water, and she gave him milk; in a bowl fit for nobles she brought him curdled milk."

Judges 5:25

Ingredients

1	3¼ oz. package vanilla instant pudding		1	8 oz. can crushed pineapple, drained
1	cup milk		⅓	cup chopped maraschino cherries
3	cup whipped topping, divided		1	graham cracker crust
2	medium bananas, sliced			

Instructions

Combine pudding mix and milk, beating until thick. Beat in 2 cups whipped topping until well combined. Fold in bananas. Pour into graham cracker crust. Top with pineapple and cherries. Chill thoroughly before serving.

TURNING THANKS

Carrie's Chocolate Pie

Carrie Dhanarajan

Ingredients

- 2 cups white sugar
- 2 tablespoons unsweetened cocoa powder
- ¼ cup all-purpose flour
- 1 12 oz. can evaporated milk
- 1 teaspoon vanilla extract
- 4 egg yolks
- ¼ cup butter
- 1 pie crust, deep dish

for meringue:
- 4 egg whites
- ¼ cup sugar

Instructions

Preheat oven to 350 degrees.

In saucepan, whisk together 2 cups sugar, cocoa, and flour. Blend in evaporated milk and vanilla. Beat egg yolks and stir into pan. Add the butter. Heat, stirring constantly, just until butter is melted. Pour filling into unbaked pie shell.

Bake in preheated oven for 35–40 minutes, or until pie is not "wobbly" when shaken.

Meringue:
Beat egg whites until soft peaks form. Gradually add ¼ cup sugar, beating constantly, until stiff peaks form. Spread meringue on pie.

Return pie to oven and bake until meringue is golden.

DESSERTS

Chocolate Pie

Sharon Sisk in Memory of Belvie and Esterline Dodson

"Eat honey, my son, for it is good; honey from the comb is sweet to your taste."

Proverbs 24:13

Ingredients
1	cup sugar	3	egg yolks
2	tablespoons cocoa	1	cup milk
2	tablespoons flour	½	stick butter

Instructions
Mix sugar, cocoa, and flour. Add beaten egg yolks, milk, and butter. Stir and cook over low heat until thick. Pour into a baked pie shell. Add meringue if desired.

TURNING THANKS

Coconut Cream Pie

In Memory of Jessie Mae Lockhart

"Keep falsehood and lies far from me; give me neither poverty nor riches, but give me only my daily bread."

Proverbs 30:8

Ingredients

- 2¼ cups milk, scalded
- 1 cup sugar
- ¼ cup cornstarch or flour
- 3 egg yolks, beaten
- ½ stick butter
- 1 teaspoon vanilla
- 1 cup coconut, canned or frozen
- 1 pie shell, baked and chilled
- 3 egg whites

Instructions

Combine milk, sugar, cornstarch, and egg yolks in a saucepan and cook until thick. Add butter, vanilla, and coconut.

Pur into a baked, chilled pie crust. Top with stiffly beaten egg whites and brown.

DESSERTS

Coconut Pie

Helen Harris

Ingredients

1	cup sugar	1	cup sweet milk
3	egg yolks (save whites for meringue)	1	tablespoon vanilla
		1	cup coconut
2	tablespoons plain flour		
½	cup sweet milk		

Instructions

Mix first 4 ingredients thoroughly; then add 1 cup sweet milk. Cook in a saucepan over medium heat until thickened.

Add vanilla and coconut and pour into baked pie shell.

Cover with meringue made from the leftover egg whites and brown in 350-degree oven.

TURNING THANKS

Buttermilk Pie

Kim Kelley

"He provides food for those who fear Him; He remembers His covenant forever."

Psalm 111:5

Ingredients

- 2 eggs
- ⅓ cup buttermilk
- ¾ cup sugar
- 1 tablespoon flour
- 1 teaspoon vanilla
- ½ stick butter, melted

Instructions

Mix flour and sugar first.

Add melted butter.

Add eggs, buttermilk, and vanilla.

Mix well and pour into an unbaked pie shell.

Bake at 275-300 degrees, depending on the oven.

Check often. When it starts to brown on top, it is done.

DESSERTS

Japanese Fruit Pie

Kay Davis

Ingredients

¾	cup sugar	½	cup coconut
1	stick butter	1	tablespoon vinegar
2	eggs	1	teaspoon vanilla
½	cup pecans	½	cup raisins

Instructions

Combine sugar and butter, add eggs and beat well.

Add pecans, coconut, raisins, vinegar, and vanilla and mix well.

Bake in unbaked pie shell for 1 hour at 300 degrees.

TURNING THANKS

Lemon Icebox Pie 1

Sarah Williams

"Peacemakers who sow in peace reap a harvest of righteousness."
James 3:18

Ingredients

- 1 small can lemonade concentrate
- 1 can Eagle brand milk
- 1 small container Cool Whip
- 1 graham cracker crust

Instructions

Stir together lemonade concentrate, Eagle brand milk, and Cool Whip by hand and pour over the graham cracker crust. Place in freezer.

DESSERTS

Lemon Icebox Pie 2

Dana Walters

Ingredients
- 1   8 oz. cream cheese (softened)
- 1   can sweetened condensed milk
- 1   teaspoon vanilla
- ⅓   cup lemon juice
- 1   container Cool Whip

Instructions
Mix cream cheese and milk together until smooth. Add vanilla and lemon juice.

Pour into prepared pie crust and top with Cool Whip.

the location of the original Akin chapel.

TURNING THANKS

Lemon Meringue Pie

Noma Jean Dodson

"John's clothes were made of camel's hair, and he had a leather belt around his waist. His food was locusts and wild honey."

Matthew 3:4

Ingredients

- 1 cup sugar
- ½ cup self-rising flour
- 3 eggs, separated
- 2 cups milk
- 2 tablespoons margarine
- 4 ounces lemon juice
- 1 cup Cool Whip
- 1 baked pie shell

Instructions

Mix sugar and flour together. Add egg yolks, milk, and lemon juice and blend well. Cook over medium heat until thick. Add margarine. Allow mixture to cool, then add Cool Whip.

Pour into prepared pie shell. Top with meringue.

DESSERTS

Lemon Cheesecake Pie

Dana Walters

Ingredients
1	8oz. cream cheese, softened	⅓	cup lemon juice
1	can sweet condensed milk	1	graham cracker pie crust
1	teaspoon vanilla	1	small container Cool Whip

Instructions
Mix cream cheese and milk with mixer, then add lemon juice and vanilla. Pour in pie crust and top with Cool Whip. Refrigerate.

Our wonderful Youth Group!

TURNING THANKS

Lemon Mousse Pie

Marilyn Peach

Ingredients

¼ cup lemon juice	1 cup sugar
1 can evaporated milk, chilled	1 box graham crackers, crushed

Instructions

Mix lemon juice, evaporated milk and sugar.

Place crushed graham crackers in the bottom of a pie pan, reserving some for top.

Pour in the mix and top with reserved crushed graham crakers.

Freeze thoroughly before serving.

DESSERTS

Cherry Cheesecake

Noma Jean Dodson

Ingredients

for the crust:

2	cups graham cracker crumbs	⅓	cup sugar
		¾	cup melted margarine

for the filling:

		1½	cups sugar
4	8 oz. packages cream cheese, softened	1	cup sour cream
		1	tablespoon vanilla

for the topping:
1   can cherry pie filling

Instructions

Crust:

Mix first 3 ingredients to make the graham cracker crust. Grease the bottom and sides of a 9" springform pan. Press graham cracker mixture firmly along the bottom and sides of the pan. Bake at 325 degrees for 15 minutes.

Filling:

Mix cream cheese until smooth, then add eggs, sugar, sour cream, and vanilla. Blend until smooth. Pour into prepared crust. Cover the outside (bottom and sides) of the springform pan with heavy duty aluminum foil, then place inside another pan about half-filled with water. Bake at 325 degrees for 1 hour. Turn off oven, but do not remove for 30 minutes. Keep refrigerated. To serve, top with cherry pie filling.

TURNING THANKS

Peanut Butter Pie

Liz Shouse Brunson

Ingredients

- 1 cup powdered sugar
- ½ cup peanut butter
- ⅔ cup sugar
- ¼ cup corn starch
- 2 cups milk
- 3 egg yolks, beaten
- 2 teaspoons butter
- ½ teaspoon vanilla
- 1 baked pie shell
- 3 egg whites (for meringue)

Instructions

Combine the powdered sugar and peanut butter. Spread ½ of the mixture on the pie shell.

Combine cornstarch, sugar, and salt. Add to scalded milk and mix well.

Pour a small amount of the milk mixture over the beaten egg yolks. Stir well, then return to the milk. Cook until thick. Add the butter and vanilla.

Pour into pie shell and top with the meringue. Sprinkle with the remainder of the peanut butter mixture.

Bake at 325 degrees until lightly browned.

Although Liz was not a regular at Mt. Wesley Akin, she would always attend dinners and activities, bringing food and laughter. Liz went to her Heavenly Home in 2011 and is missed by everyone.

DESSERTS

Strawberry Pie 1

Noma Jean Dodson

Ingredients

- ¾ cup sugar
- 3 tablespoons corn starch
- 1½ cups water
- 1 3 oz. package strawberry gelatin
- strawberries, fresh, cut into halves — enough to fill pie shell
- 1 baked pie shell

Instructions

In a saucepan combine sugar, corn starch, and water. Bring to a boil and cook until thick.

Remove from heat and stir in gelatin until dissolved. Chill until partially set.

Mix in strawberries. Put in a pre-cooked pie shell and refrigerate until set.

TURNING THANKS

Strawberry Pie 2

Carol Walters

Ingredients

- 1 regular box strawberry Jell-O
- 3 tablespoons flour (heaping)
- ¾ cup sugar or Splenda
- 1¼ cup water
- 1 uncooked pie crust, baked or graham cracker crust
- 2+ cups strawberries

Instructions

Mix water, sugar, and flour and bring to a boil. Add Jell-O and stir until thickened. Let mixture cool.

Pour mixture over strawberries in a large bowl, mix and pour into the baked crust or graham crust. Add Cool Whip if desired or ice cream.

This recipe can be easily doubled, and can be made the day before to carry to a meal.

DESSERTS

Brown Sugar Brownies

Marie Vestal Walters

"You were bought at a price. Therefore honor God with your bodies."

1 Corinthians 6:20

Ingredients

1	stick butter	2	teaspoons baking powder
1 ½	cup brown sugar packed		
2	eggs	½ to 1	cup nuts, chopped
1	teaspoon vanilla	1	cup dry coconut
1 ½	cup flour		

Instructions

Grease a 13 x 9 x 2" pan. Melt butter in a saucepan, remove from heat, add sugar, and blend. Add eggs one at a time, beating well, stir in vanilla, flour, and baking powder. Mix thoroughly.

Add nuts and coconut. Stir lightly to combine. Pour into greased pan.

Bake 30 minutes at 350 degrees, do not over bake.

Cool in pan and cut into squares.

TURNING THANKS

Brownies

Noma Jean Dodson

"Taste and see that the LORD is good; blessed is the one who takes refuge in him."

Psalms 34:8

Ingredients

1	cup all-purpose flour plus 2 tablespoons	⅓	cup baking cocoa
⅔	cup brown sugar	½	cup walnuts
¾	teaspoon salt	3	eggs
⅔	cup sugar	⅔	cup vegetable oil
1	teaspoon baking powder	1	teaspoon vanilla

Instructions

Combine flour, salt, baking powder, and cocoa. Mix sugars, eggs, and oil and combine with the flour mixture. Stir in walnuts and vanilla.

Cook in a 350 degree preheated oven till a toothpick comes out clean.

DESSERTS

Pumpkin Pie Bars

Paula Rozelle Hanback

Ingredients

1⅓	cups flour	1	cup old-fashioned or quick-cooking oats, uncooked
½	cup firmly packed brown sugar		
¾	cup granulated sugar, divided	½	cup chopped pecans
¾	cup (1½ sticks) cold butter or margarine	1	8 oz. package cream cheese, softened
		3	eggs
		1	15 oz. can pumpkin
		1	tablespoon pumpkin pie spice

Instructions

Preheat oven to 350 degrees. Line 13 x 9" baking pan with foil; grease foil lining. Mix flour, brown sugar, and ¼ cup of the granulated sugar in medium bowl; cut in butter with pastry blender or 2 knives until mixture resembles coarse crumbs. Stir in oats and pecans. Reserve 1 cup of the oat mixture; press remaining mixture onto bottom of pan. Bake 15 min.

Beat cream cheese, remaining ½ cup sugar, eggs, pumpkin, and pumpkin pie spice in small bowl with electric mixer on medium speed until well blended. Pour over crust; sprinkle with reserved crumb mixture.

Bake 25 min. Lift from pan using foil; cool completely. Cut into 24 bars. Refrigerate leftovers.

TURNING THANKS

Pumpkin Cheesecake Bars

Ramona Robertson

Ingredients

- 1 16 oz. package pound cake mix
- 3 eggs
- 2 tablespoons butter, melted
- 4 teaspoons pumpkin pie spice
- 1 8 oz. package cream cheese, softened
- 1 can Eagle Brand milk
- 1 16 oz. can pumpkin (not pie mix)
- ½ teaspoon salt
- 1 cup chopped nuts (pecans or walnuts)

Instructions

On low speed, mix cake mix, 1 egg, 2 teaspoons pumpkin spice mix, and butter until crumbly. Press into 15 x 10" baking dish to form a crust.

In another bowl, beat cream cheese until fluffy. Gradually add Eagle Brand milk, 2 eggs, pumpkin, 2 teaspoons pumpkin pie spice, and salt. Mix well.

Pour over crust; sprinkle with nuts. Bake 30 to 35 minutes at 350 degrees.

Cool and refrigerate at least 8 hours before cutting.

DESSERTS

Death-by-Caramel Squares

Shirley Hanback

Ingredients

2	cups light brown sugar, firmly packed	1	teaspoon baking powder
2	cups unsalted butter, melted	½	teaspoon baking soda
3	eggs, large, lightly beaten	¼	teaspoon salt
1	tablespoon vanilla extract	6	2.07 oz. Snickers bars, chopped
4	cups all-purpose flour	1	14 oz. can *dulce de leche* (thick caramel-like milk base spread)
1	cup uncooked regular oats		

Instructions

Combine brown sugar, butter, eggs, and vanilla extract. Stir until well-blended. Add flour, oats, baking powder, and baking soda. Stir until well-blended, then add Snickers bars.

Cover a 9 x 13" baking pan in aluminum foil and coat foil with non-stick cooking spray. Pour batter into pan. Dollop dulce de leche on top of batter and use a knife to swirl into batter.

Bake for 65 minutes at 325 degrees. After baking, cool in the pan on a wire rack for several hours. When completely cool, remove from pan and cut into squares.

TURNING THANKS

Tea Cakes

In Memory of Tommye Haywood

Ingredients

1	cup sugar	1	egg
½	teaspoon salt	1	teaspoon vanilla
¾	cup butter	1	teaspoon baking powder

Instructions

Cream together sugar and butter. Add egg and vanilla and continue mixing well.

Add flour, kneading until a stiff dough is formed. Chill dough and roll out until very thin.

Sprinkle with sugar and cut out using your favorite cookie cutters. Bake in a 350 degree oven until brown.

Tommye is the mother of Frances Fraser and the wife of Bro. James Hubert Haywood.

DESSERTS

Butterfinger Cookies

Noma Jean Dodson

Ingredients

½	cup shortening or magarine	1	cup all-purpose flour
¾	cup sugar	½	teaspoon baking soda
2	eggs	¼	teaspoon salt
1¼	cup peanut butter, creamy or chunky	5	butterfinger candy bars, chopped
½	teaspoon vanilla	⅔	cup brown sugar

Instructions

Cream shortening or margarine and sugars until fluffy.

Beat in eggs, stir in peanut butter and vanilla.

Combine flour, baking soda, and salt, then add to the creamed mixture.

Add chopped candy bars.

Spoon on a greased baking sheet 2 inches apart.

Bake at 350 degrees until golden brown.

TURNING THANKS

Hay Stack Cookies

Frances Haywood Woodall Fraser

Ingredients
- 2 cups graham cracker crumbs
- 1 stick butter or margarine
- 2 cups sugar
- ½ cup Pet milk
- 20 marshmallows, large
- 1 cup coconut
- 1 cup nuts

Instructions
Cream sugar and butter, add milk and cook for 3 minutes

Add marshmallows and stir until dissolved.

Remove from heat and add cracker crumbs, coconut and nuts. Blend well.

Drop by spoon on wax paper.

Miss Frances joined the church in 1930.

DESSERTS

Sugar Cookies

Marie Vestal Walters

"He provides food for the cattle and for the young ravens when they call."

Psalm 147:9

Ingredients

1	cup granulated sugar	2	eggs, well beaten
1	cup powdered sugar	2	teaspoons vanilla
1	cup magarine, softened	1	teaspoon soda
1	cup oil	1	teaspoon cream of tartar
5¾	cups flour, plain		

Instructions

Cream sugars with magarine. Add eggs, stir in vanilla and oil.

Mix in the dry ingrdients and blend well. Refrigerate overnight.

Form into balls and put on a cookie sheet. Dip the bottom of a glass in granulated sugar and mash down balls.

Bake at 350 degrees for 10–12 minutes.

This cookie dough can be kept in the refrigerator and cooked as needed.

TURNING THANKS

The Cookie Jar Recipe

Shirley Hanback

Ingredients

2½	cups flour	1	cup granulated sugar
1	teaspoon baking soda	1	cup packed brown sugar
½	teaspoon salt	2	eggs
1	cup Parkay spread sticks (2 sticks)	2	teaspoon vanilla

Instructions

Mix flour, baking soda and salt in a small bowl.

Beat butter spread and sugars in a large bowl until fluffy. Blend in eggs and vanilla.

Add flour mixture, beating until blended.

Stir in *variations* of your choice.

Drop by rounded tablespoons onto ungreased cookie sheets. Bake at 375 degrees for 8 to 10 minutes. Cool 2 minutes. Remove from cookie sheets and cool on wire racks. Makes 5 dozen.

DESSERTS

Variations:

Chunky Chocolate Chip Cookies: Stir in 2 cups Baker's Semi Sweet real chocolate chips.

Double Chocolate Brownie Cookies: Mix ½ cup unsweetened cocoa with flour mixture. Stir in 2 cups semi sweet real chocolate chips.

Raisin Cookies: Stir in 2 cups dark raisins or yogurt covered raisins or chocolate covered raisins.

Applesauce Oatmeal: Stir in ⅓ cup applesauce and 1 ½ cups uncooked oatmeal.

Peanut butter and Chocolate Chip: Mix ½ cup peanut butter with Parkay. Stir in 2 cups milk chocolate chips.

TURNING THANKS

Chocolate Oatmeal Cookies

Agnes Williams

Ingredients

- 2 cups sugar
- ½ cup margarine
- ⅓ cup cocoa
- ½ cup milk
- ½ cup peanut butter
- 1 teaspoon vanilla
- 3 cups instant oatmeal

Instructions

Bring to a boil sugar, margarine, cocoa, and milk. Cool 1 minute. Remove from heat and add peanut butter, vanilla, and oats. Mix and spoon onto wax paper.

Nuts may be added if desired.

DESSERTS

Date Nut Balls

Barbara Keltner

Ingredients
- 2 cups butter or margarine
- ¼ cup sugar
- 1 8 oz. package chopped dates
- ½ cup Rice Krispies cereal
- 1 cup chopped pecans

Instructions
Combine butter, sugar, and dates in a saucepan. Bring to a boil, cook, stirring constantly for three minutes.

Stir in cereal and pecans, cool to touch. Shape into 1" balls and roll in coconut or powdered sugar. Yields 4 dozen.

If mixture is too thick, add white syrup.

*This is a good Christmas recipe.

TURNING THANKS

Divinity Candy

Marie Vestal Walters

"But food does not bring us near to God; we are no worse if we do not eat, and no better if we do."

1 Corinthians 8:8

Ingredients

2½	cups sugar	½	cup white corn syrup
½	cup water	2	egg whites
2	teaspoons vanilla	1	cup nuts

Instructions

Mix sugar, syrup, and water and boil until a hard ball forms when dropped in cold water.

Have egg whites beaten and pour the boiled mixture over the whites. While pouring over the egg whites, keep stirring. Add vanilla and keep beating. Add nuts last, just before spooning out. Spoon out on wax paper 1 teaspoon at a time.

DESSERTS

Peanut Butter Balls
Shirley Hanback

Ingredients
1	10 oz. jar peanut butter (creamy or crunchy)	1⅓	sticks softened margarine
		1	box powdered sugar

Instructions
Cream together peanut butter and margarine. Add powdered sugar. Roll into walnut-sized balls and dip in melted chocolate coating purchased from your grocery. You can make your own coating mixture by following the instructions below:

Chocolate Coating:
Melt ½ bar paraffin and one 12 oz. package milk chocolate chips in double boiler. Dip balls in chocolate, using a toothpick. Cool on waxed paper. Cover the toothpick hole with a drop of chocolate.

TURNING THANKS

Marcille's Nutty Fudge Candy

In Memory of Marcille Love

Ingredients

- 5 cups sugar
- 2 sticks butter
- 1 large can Pet milk
- 1 12 oz. package chocolate morsels
- 1 pint marshmallow whip
- 2 teaspoons vanilla
- 3 cups nuts

Instructions

Mix sugar, butter and Pet milk in a large sauce pan. Bring to boil, stirring constantly to prevent sticking.

Turn heat down after a constant boil is reached and cook until soft ball stage is reached.

Remove from heat and add chocolate morsels, marshmallow whip, vanilla, and nuts. Beat a few minutes and pour into a greased baking pan or dish. Let cool overnight.

Cut in thin slices because it is very rich. To complete this candy it should take 8 minutes. If overcooked it becomes grainy.

DESSERTS

Creamy Pralines

Janis Rozelle

Ingredients

- 1 lb. light brown sugar
- 1 6 oz. can evaporated milk
- 2 tablespoons light Karo syrup
- ¼ cup butter
- 1 teaspoon vanilla
- 1½ cups pecan halves

Instructions

Cook sugar, milk, and corn syrup in 2-quart saucepan over medium heat, stirring constantly until mixture comes to a boil.

Cook, stirring constantly, until temperature reaches 238 degrees on a candy thermometer (soft ball stage). Remove from heat. Add butter. Do not stir.

Cool to 110 degrees. Add vanilla and beat until creamy. Stir in pecans.

Drop by tablespoons onto wax paper and cool.

In New Orleans, Santa gets a plate of pralines, not cookies!

TURNING THANKS

Peach Ice Cream

In Memory of Bracken Walters, Jr.

Ingredients
- 1 quart peaches, fresh or frozen
- 2½ cups sugar
- 2 teaspoon vanilla
- 1 gallon milk

Instructions
Blend the peaches in a food processor or blender.

Add all other ingredients and place in the ice cream freezer.

Churn until it will not move.

Mr. Bracken would make this homemade ice cream all summer long. When he had his orchard, he used his home grown peaches and had to freeze in a hand cranked churn. It was well worth the work!

DESSERTS

Ice Cream
Dana Walters

Ingredients
6	eggs, separated	4	tablespoons flour
1	can sweetened condensed milk	2	tablespoons vanilla milk
1⅓	cups sugar		

Instructions
Mix sugar, flour, egg yolks, and condensed milk. Cream together.

Beat egg whites until stiff.

Pour egg yolk mixture in container, fold in vanilla and egg whites. Add any fresh fruit if desired. Finish filling container with milk.

Put in electric freezer. Put a layer of ice and then a layer of ice cream salt, until freezer is full. When freezer stops running, unplug and cover with a towel until cream hardens.

TURNING THANKS

Cherry Supreme Dessert

Carol Walters

Ingredients
- 1 angel food cake, cut into approximately 1-inch pieces
- 2 cans of Bing cherry pie filling
- 1 large package vanilla instant pudding, prepared according to package directions
- 1 large Cool Whip

Instructions

1st layer—place ½ of the pieces of angel food cake in the bottom of clear trifle bowl.

2nd layer—mix the pudding according to package instructions; pour ½ over angel food cake layer.

3rd layer—pour ½ cherry pie filling over pudding.

4th layer—cover pie filling with ½ Cool Whip

Repeat layers, ending with Cool Whip on top.

Variation: Other fruits or pie fillings are optional.

*Very Delicious! Will keep several days, makes a pretty dish.

DESSERTS

Strawberry Pizza

Marie Vestal Walters

Ingredients

for the crust:

1½	cups plain flour	¼	cup brown sugar
1	cup chopped pecans	1	cup melted margarine

for the filling:

1	8 oz. package cream cheese, softened	1	12 oz. container Cool Whip
		2	cups confectioners sugar

for the topping:

1	cup sugar	1	3 oz. package strawberry Jell-O
2	tablespoons corn starch		
1½	cups water	4	cups sliced strawberries

Instructions

Crust
Mix all ingredients together and press in 9 x 13" pan. Bake at 400 degrees for 15 minutes and cool.

Filling
Mix cream cheese and sugar until well blended. Fold in Cool Whip. Spread mixture on crust.

Topping
Mix sugar, corn starch, and water. Cook until thickened. Stir in Jell-O. Allow mixture to cool, then mix with strawberries. Spread on top of filling. Refrigerate.

TURNING THANKS

Strawberry Trifle

Noma Jean Dodson

Ingredients

for the cake layer:
- 1 yellow or white cake mix, prepared according to package directions

for the strawberry layer:
- 1 quart fresh sliced strawberries
- 1 13.6 oz. container of strawberry glaze

for the pudding layer:
- 1 cup sugar
- ½ cup self-rising flour
- 3 egg yolks
- 2 cups milk
- 1 teaspoon vanilla
- 2 tablespoons margarine

for topping:
- 1 container Cool Whip

Instructions

Layer as follows in a 9 x 13" dish

Cake Layer:
Bake yellow or white cake mix by instructions on the box. Cool. Cut in cubes. Line the bottom of the dish with cake cubes. You will not need all the cake.

DESSERTS

Pudding Layer:
Mix sugar and flour, stir in egg yolks and milk. Cook until smooth enough to spread. Stir in vanilla and margarine. Cool and spread over cake cubes.

Strawberry Layer:
Mix together and spread on top of pudding layer.

Topping:
Top with a layer of Cool Whip.

The Sanctuary

TURNING THANKS

Quick Fudge Pudding

Gail Pigg

Ingredients
for the batter:

2	tablespoons margarine	2	tablespoons cocoa
1	cup self-rising flour	½	cup sweet milk
¾	cup sugar	1	teaspoon vanilla

for the sauce:

¾	cup brown sugar	1¾	cup hot water
¼	cup cocoa		

Instructions
Preheat the oven to 350 degrees.

Melt the magarine in a 8½ x 9" baking dish.

Combine the milk, cocoa, and vanilla in a mixing bowl and pour over the margarine.

Sauce:
Mix the sauce ingredients and pour over the cake batter.

Bake at 350 degrees until the cake is firm.

Sauce will be on the bottom of the cake.

Gail's mother, Mary Rountree, used to make this quick dessert for her family.

DESSERTS

Cream Cheese Pastry

Dana Walters

Ingredients

2	cans crescent rolls (8 each)	1	stick margarine, melted
16	oz. cream cheese, softened	1	teaspoon cinnamon
1¼	cups sugar	¼	cup sugar
1	teaspoon vanilla		

Instructions

Unroll 1 can of rolls on bottom of 9 x 13" dish (do not press seams together).

Mix cream cheese, 1 ¼ cup sugar, and vanilla together. Spread over rolls.

Unroll second can of rolls on top of mixture. Pour melted butter over top of rolls. Mix ¼ cup sugar and cinnamon together and sprinkle on top of butter.

Bake at 350 degrees for 20 minutes.

TURNING THANKS

Popcorn Balls

Marie Vestal Walters

Ingredients
- 3 quarts popped corn
- ½ teaspoon salt
- 1 tablespoon butter
- 1 cup molasses
- ½ cup sugar

Instructions
Pop corn and put in a large pan. Sprinkle with salt and set aside.

Melt butter in a large sauce pan, then add molasses and sugar. Cook over medium heat until it reaches the hard ball stage when tested in cold water. Pour mixture over the popcorn gradually, while stirring the corn constantly. Using your hands, shape into balls, using as little pressure as possible.

Wrap each ball individually in plastic wrap and tie with ribbon.

Popcorn Balls were a staple on Halloween Night when trick-or-treating at Miss Marie's.

DESSERTS

Caramel Corn

Carol Walters

Ingredients

2	cups brown sugar	1	teaspoon soda
2	sticks butter or magarine	12	cups popped corn
½	cup white corn syrup	1	cup peanuts
1	teaspoon salt		

Instructions

Pop corn. Combine brown sugar, butter, corn syrup, and salt. Boil for 5 minutes over medium heat. Stir in soda and pour quickly over popped corn. Stir in peanuts and pour into 2 large greased baking pans.

Bake at 250 degrees for 1 hour, stirring every 15 minutes. Cool and continue to stir. Store in a tight container.

TURNING THANKS

Chocolate Gravy

Robbie Fox

"And because of the abundance of the milk they give, he will have curds to eat. All who remain in the land will eat curds and honey."

Isaiah 7:22

Ingredients

1	tablespoon cocoa	½	cup water
½	cup sugar	1	tablespoon butter
1	tablespoon flour		

Instructions

Stir cocoa, sugar, and flour. Add water and butter and stir. Cook on medium heat until thick.

Serve over biscuits.

DESSERTS

Chocolate Rolls
Janie Fox

Ingredients
for syrup:
- 2 cups water
- 2 tablespoons cocoa
- 1 cup sugar
- ½ cup butter

for rolls:
- 1 cup flour
- ½ cup sugar
- ½ cup milk
- 1 teaspoon vanilla

Instructions
Mix the water, cocoa, 1 cup sugar, ½ cup butter together and bring to a boil. Pour into a baking dish.

Mix the flour, ½ cup sugar, milk, and vanilla and drop by spoon into the chocolate mix.

Bake at 350 degrees until rolls are lightly browned.

Janie's family was part of the Mission Baptist Church on Akin Ridge that later became Akin Chapel Church of the Nazarene.

NOTES

NOTES

NOTES

NOTES

HELPFUL HINTS

Use Lifesavers candy to hold candles in place on your next birthday cake.

Stuff a miniature marshmallow in the bottom of a sugar cone to prevent ice cream drips.

Zap garlic cloves in the microwave for 15 seconds and the skins slip right off.

Use a meat baster to "squeeze" your pancake batter onto the hot griddle. Perfectly shaped pancakes every time.

Always spray your grill with nonstick cooking spray before grilling to avoid sticking.

To keep potatoes from budding, place an apple in the bag with the potatoes.

To prevent egg shells from cracking, add a pinch of salt to water before hard-boiling.

Use a pastry blender to cut ground beef into small pieces after browning.

Sweeten whipped cream with confectioner's sugar instead of granulated sugar. It will stay fluffy and hold its shape better.

For easy "meatloaf" mixing, combine the ingredients with a potato masher.

If you don't have enough batter to fill all cupcake tins, pour 1 tablespoon of water into the unfilled spots. This helps preserve the life of your pans.

To easily remove honey from a measuring spoon, first coat the spoon with nonstick cooking spray.

Run your hands under cold water before pressing Rice Krispies Treats in the pan The marshmallow won't stick to your fingers.

Mash and freeze ripe bananas, in one-cup portions, for use in later baking. No wasted bananas. Or you can freeze them whole, peeled, in plastic baggies.

To quickly use that frozen juice concentrate, simply mash it with a potato masher. No need to wait for it to thaw.

To get the most juice out of fresh lemons, bring them to room temperature and roll them under your palm against the kitchen counter before squeezing.

To easily remove burnt-on food from your skillet, simply add a drop or two of dish soap and enough water to cover bottom of pan, and bring to a boil on stovetop. Skillet will be much easier to clean now.

Spray your Tupperware with nonstick cooking spray before pouring in tomato-based sauces. No more stains.

Transfer your jelly to a small plastic squeeze bottle. No more messy, sticky, jars or knives. This also works well for homemade salad dressing.

To aid in washing dishes, add a tablespoon of baking soda to your soapy water. It softens hands while cutting through grease.

Save your store-bought bread bags and ties. They make perfect storage bags for homemade bread.

When a cake recipe calls for flouring the baking pan, use a bit of the dry cake mix instead. No white mess on the outside of the cake.

If you accidentally over-salt a dish while it's still cooking, drop in a peeled potato. It absorbs the excess salt for an instant "fix me up."

Next time you need a quick ice pack, grab a bag of frozen vegetables out of your freezer. No watery leaks from a plastic baggie.

When making bread, substitute nondairy creamer for the dry milk. It works just as well.

Rinse cooked, ground meat with water when draining off the fat. This helps "wash away" even more fat.

Slicing meat when partially frozen makes it easier to get thin slices.

Instead of throwing away bread heels or leftover cornbread, use them to make bread crumbs. For use later, store them in the freezer.

Wrap celery in aluminum foil when putting in the refrigerator. It will keep for weeks.

Substitute half applesauce for the vegetable oil in your baking recipes. You will greatly reduce the fat content. (Example: ½ cup vegetable oil = ¼ cup applesauce + ¼ cup oil)

To ripen avocados and bananas, enclose them in a brown paper bag with an apple for 2-3 days.

Brush beaten egg white over pie crust before baking for a beautiful glossy finish.

In recipes calling for margarine, substitute reduced calorie margarine to help cut back on fat. (Same for sour cream, milk, cheese, cream cheese, and cream soups.)

Place a slice of bread in hardened brown sugar to soften it back up.

When boiling corn on the cob, add a pinch of sugar to help bring out the corn's natural sweetness.

When starting your garden seedlings indoors, plant the seeds in egg shell halves. Simply crack the shells around the roots of your plants and transplant them outdoors. The shell is a natural fertilizer.

To determine whether an egg is fresh, immerse it in a pan of cool, salted water. If it sinks, it is fresh. If it rises to the surface, throw it away.

Keep the linings from cereal boxes. They make great substitutes for waxed paper.

A Brief History of
Mt. Wesley Akin Nazarene Church
1878—2011 (133 Years)

compiled by James R. Hanback, Sr.

TURNING THANKS

Ministers of the Santa Fe Circuit and Mt. Wesley Akin Nazarene Church

1878–1918 — Rev. William O. Roberts and R. G. Linn (Missionary Methodists)
1911–1917 — Rev. S. W. McGowan was one of the first circuit ministers. Akin Church started before Mt. Wesley.
1917–1921 — Rev. E. T. Cox
1921–1923 — Rev. G. W. Pirtle
1924–1925 — Rev. L. Brooks Matthews
1925–1926 — Rev. F. G. Baine
1926–1927 — Rev. Chester Wilkinson
1927–1928 — Rev. S. A. Jones
1929–1931 — Rev. L. Brooks Matthews
1931–1939 — Rev. G. E. Pirtle
1939–1943 — Rev. Marcus E. Perkins
1943–1973 — Rev. E. P. Boyett
1973–1986 — Rev. Dr. Johnny J. Wheelbarger
1987–1990 — Rev. Henderson Goins
1990–1998 — Pastor Kenvin Sisk
2002–Pres. — Rev. David Usry

HISTORY

Akin Chapel 1908-1987

The Missionary Baptists erected a chapel two miles west of Water Valley in 1896. It cost them about $300. The building was located on what is now called Akin Ridge Road near the schoolhouse, which was then known as Akin Academy. The schoolhouse was named for A. N. Akin, who donated the school bell.

Akin Academy was erected in 1886 at cost of $500 on land donated by Dallas Alexander.

A transcription of the original deed as it was written (framed and displayed in the church lobby) follows.

State of Tennessee, Maury County
District no. 1

For and in consideration of $100.00 paid in repairs we the trustees, T. C. Harris, W. H. Beasley, Henry Brown of Mission Chapel the Baptist Church located on the ridge near Akins School house do hereby transfer a half interest of the said church properties to the trustees of the Pentecostal Mission, J. M. Dodson, W. M. Harbison, A. C. Letsinger or their successors to have and to hold and to use as they may see proper for public worship and have a right and privilege to use the church half the time and we the trustees of the second part do agree to straten up the place brace it as best we can and paint it and fence the yard and when any repairing is to be done both partys will do their

TURNING THANKS

part and we the trustees of the first part T. C. Harris, W. H. Beasley, Henry Brown do hereby warrant and defend the title of said church property against the claims of every person whomsoever for witness we have hereunto subscribed our names and affixed our seals this the 10th day of Sep 1909.

J. H. Brown
W. J. Peach
E. C. Harris
(Born one mile north of Williamsport on April 5, 1860)
W. H. Beasley

The trustees of the Pentecostal Mission (later to become Akin Chapel Church of the Nazarene) were:
J. M. Dodson *(Born two miles east of Santa Fe on Jan. 6, 1846)*
William M. Harbison *(Born at Water Valley on Jan. 13, 1840)*
A.C. Letsinger

This deed was not filed until November 7, 1910 at 9:30 AM.

HISTORY

The official organization of the Akin Pentecostal Church of the Nazarene was not until the early part of 1911. Seventeen (17) charter members were enrolled at the start. The Rev. S. R. McGowan was pastor.

S. R. McGowan, A. J. Miller, J. M. Dodson and A. C. Letsinger were elected as board members with S. R. McGowan serving as the Sunday School Superintendent.

The Tennessee District Church of the Nazarene traces its roots to the spring of 1911 when Hiram F. Reynolds, general superintendent of the Church of the Nazarene, appointed the Rev. J. J. Rye as the founding district superintendent of the first fully established work in the state of Tennessee, The Clarksville District Church of the Nazarene. In October of 1911, Reynolds established the Southeast Tennessee District, headquartered in Water Valley, Tennessee.

S. R. McGowan was appointed as the new district superintendent. The Second District Assembly (Southeast District) was held October 10–13, 1912, at the Akin Church. The Rev. S. R. McGowan was district superintendent. H. F. Reynolds was the general superintendent. The meeting was called to order at 9:30 AM. The hymn *I'm On My Way to Heaven* was sung. There was a prayer and then a scripture reading from Romans 12.

TURNING THANKS

Akin Chapel was a part of the Water Valley Circuit along with the Fly and Sawdust churches. The parsonage was located in Water Valley and remained there through until April 1927, when a fire destroyed it. A new parsonage was purchased for $962.50. It was located just off the Square in Santa Fe and remains there to this day. When the new parsonage was purchased, the circuit changed to the Santa Fe Circuit, which at the time included the churches of Hilltown, Akin Chapel, Mt. Wesley, and Fly.

Akin Chapel continued to meet in the building that had been purchased in 1910 until 1967, when the State of Tennessee condemned the property to build the Natchez Trace Parkway. The original church building was west of Water Valley on Akin Ridge Road, which runs in close proximity to the Natchez Trace Parkway. The Akin Ridge Nazarene Church Cemetery (also called the Akin Academy Cemetery) remains located about 100 yards away from the New Natchez Trace Parkway on the right side of the road.

The Akin Church then purchased the Alexander Methodist Church, which was not being used at the time, for $500.

The Alexander Methodist Church, also called the Water Valley Methodist Church, was built in 1883 on land donated by G. M. D. and Eben Alexander. The church was named in honor of them. The building is located about a half-mile west of Water Valley Community and resides on the same lot as the Alexandria Cemetery.

Akin Chapel continued to meet at their new location until December of 1987 when Akin and Mt. Wesley decided to merge in order to better serve the Lord.

HISTORY

Mt. Wesley: the Beginning 1841–1878

M. E. Churches, South
Robert's Chapel—In 1841 Merrett Sedberry donated to church purposes the site of the above chapel, and a class was organized as follows: Mr. Sedberry, John Smith, James K. Gardner, James Brazwell, William Roberts, Jenkins Scanlin.

The M. E. denomination divided on political grounds, and M. E. Church, South, was organized, 1846, at Roberts' Bend, with 25 or more members, and was served by pastors from Duck River and Santa Fe Circuits until 1880. A mission church was organized, with 7 members, 1878, and ministered by R. G. Lynn[1], W. O. Roberts and others in the same meetinghouse[2].

Mt. Wesley, northwest of the above was organized with 66 members in recent years, and a site purchased by the Methodist Missionary Society from L. Anderson. Pastors have been the same as at Roberts' Chapel.

(Transcribed from Century Review of Maury County, Tennessee 1807-1907 reprinted by the Maury County Historical Society. Original publication was 1905, pages 232-233.)

The Methodists continued to hold church services at Mt. Wesley until 1918 when it was sold to the Pentecostal Church of the

---

1. The spelling of R. G. Lynn is given as R. G. Linn from a September 20, 1923, edition of the *Maury Democrat* newspaper obituary for the Rev. William O. Roberts.

2. It appears from other records and deeds that the Mt. Wesley building, a one-room structure with outhouse, was erected between 1878 and 1880.

TURNING THANKS

Nazarene. The Rev. William O. Roberts served as the primary pastor.

The Methodist and Nazarene Churches are based on the philosophy and doctrine of John Wesley. With this common ground one could say that Reverend Roberts, who founded the Mt. Wesley Methodist church, also founded the Mt. Wesley Church of the Nazarene. Many of the Methodist church members remained in attendance at Mt. Wesley Nazarene, although some did not transfer their membership. Two known attendees were Jerome R. Vestal and Mrs. Rose Anna Adams Vestal.

HISTORY

Mt. Wesley Nazarene Church: 1918

On Dec. 6, 1918, the Board of Trustees of the Pentecostal Church of the Nazarene purchased the Mt. Wesley property from The Missionary Methodist Church.

A transcription of the original deed (framed and displayed in the church lobby) follows.

State of Tennessee
Maury County

For and in consideration of the sum of six hundred dollars ($600.00) paid and to be paid as follows:

Three hundred dollars ($300.00) cash in hand the receipt of which is hereby acknowledged, and three hundred dollars ($300.00) evidenced by promissory note of C. F. Church, J. H. Haywood, J. H. Younger, J. M. Hood and G. W. Haywood trustees of the Pentecostal Church of the Nazarene, said note being of even date with this instrument, bearing interest from date, and due one year from date, and secured by a lien expressly retained on the property hereinafter transferred and conveyed, we, J. M. Roberts, A. P. Roberts, J. R. Vestal, W. O. Roberts, and Sidney Adams, Trustees of The Missionary Methodist, in whom is vested as Trustees the title to the hereinafter described property, have this day bargained and sold

TURNING THANKS

and do by these presents transfer and convey to the above named Trustees of The Pentecostal Church of The Nazarene the following described property, located and situated in the Second Civil District of Maury County, Tenn., lying on the Columbia, and Santa Fe Turnpike about seven miles from the City of Columbia, Tennessee, and being that property which was deeded to The Trustees of The Missionary Methodist Church by L. Anderson and wife, by deed registered in the Register's office of Maury County, Tenn., comprising one acre, more or less, on which is now built a house of Worship; This property as a whole is bounded on the N. by the Columbia & Santa Fe Turnpike, on the E. and S. by J. R. Vestal; and on the W. by Jas. M. Gregory; but it is distinctly understood and agreed that there is reserved a part of this one acre, for the purpose of a Burial Ground on the Southern end of this lot, the part reserved being cut off the Southern end by a line drawn parallel with the Southern end of said Church, and within three feet of the said Church and all that South of the said line being not transferred and conveyed in this instrument but expressly retained and reserved for the said purpose.

To have and to hold them the said Trustees, their assigns and successors, now and forever together with all the right, title, interest, estate, claims, easements,

HISTORY

appurtenances and hereditaments thereunto pertaining and belonging.

And we covenant with the said Trustees their assigns and successors, that we are lawfully seized and possessed of this property, that we have a good right to convey the same, that it is unencumbered; and we bind ourselves, our assigns and or successors to forever warrant and defend the title to the same against the lawful demands of all persons whomsoever.

I, L. Anderson, original grantor sign this deed for the purpose of releasing and quit claiming all right, title, interest that I may have had in way to this property.

This Nov. 30, 1918

                 A. P. Roberts Jr *(Anderson)*
                 J. R. Vestal *(Jerome R. Vestal)*
                     R. M. Roberts
                     Sidney Adams
                   W. O. Roberts *(William O.)*
                        L. Anderson

Filed on December 6, 1918

TURNING THANKS

Notes:
J. H. Younger (John Howard) is the grandfather of current member Norma Ann Jones.
J. H. Haywood (James Hubert) is the father of current member Frances Haywood Woodall Fraser.
J. R. Vestal (Jerome) is the grandfather of current member Marie Vestal Walters.
Sidney Adams (Albert Sidney Johnston) is the uncle of current member Marie Vestal Walters.
J. M. Hood is Johnny Hood and G. W. Haywood is George Haywood.

Trivia note: There is a lot of reference to the Santa Fe Circuits for several denominations in historical records. Santa Fe was originally known as Benton, but the United States Post Office already had records for a Benton, Tennessee. In November, 1849, the name was changed to Santa Fe, Tennessee. Not to be confused with other places having the name Santa Fe, the locals pronounce it as **San-tuh-Fee** *instead of* **San-tuh-Fay.** *"Santa Fe" literally means "Holy Faith" in Spanish, which could explain the multitude of churches throughout the area.*

HISTORY

Timeline

1918	The Rev. S. W. McGowan was one of first circuit ministers. McGowan was the District Superintendent for the Southeast Tennessee District. The district was found in October, 1911 and headquarter in Water Valley, Tennessee.

1929	Hilltown Pentecostal Church of the Nazarene. The original church was started as a Missionary Methodist church by the Rev. William O. Roberts, the founder of the original Mt. Wesley church.

1930	The Rev. L. Brooks Matthews

1939	The Rev. Marcus E. Perkins

1943—1973	The Rev. E. P. Boyett is appointed pastor for the Santa Fe Circuit. Rev. Boyett and his wife Lottie retired on August 12, 1973, after 30 years of service. During those 30 years, Rev. Boyett received 208 members into the Church of the Nazarene. The Santa Fe circuit consisted of Mt. Wesley, Akin Chapel, Hilltown, Elmore, and Fly Churches.

1945	Hilltown Church becomes part of the Santa Fe circuit.

TURNING THANKS

1959   Elmore Church organized.

1965   Mt. Wesley building remodeled. Contoured slat wood pews, hardwood floor, sheetrock and paint, and electric heat were added. There was no air conditioning. The first wedding to be held in the remodeled church was that of Shirley A. Walters and James R. Hanback on June 5, 1965. The Rev E. P. Boyett officiated.

1968   Added Sunday School rooms to building.

1973   The Rev. E. P. Boyett and Lottie retire after 30 years.

1973–1986 The Rev. Dr. Johnny J. Wheelbarger and Bonnie

1987–1990 The Rev. Henderson Goins

1987   Mt. Wesley and Akin Chapel merge into Mt. Wesley Akin Nazarene Church. Akin Chapel vacated their building because of the construction of the Natchez Trace Parkway. Akin was originally built in 1908 under a Pentecostal denomination, but in 1911 became part of the Nazarene denomination.

1988   Building annex added to existing building.

HISTORY

1990   Mt. Wesley Akin Church left the Santa Fe circuit and hired a full time pastor.

1990   Pastor Kenvin Sisk

1990   Fellowship Hall built.

2002   The Rev. David Usry and Michelle

2010   Pastor: the Rev. David Usry.

             Board members: Larry Fox, Janie Fox, Jeff Fox, Donnise Clark, Marilyn Peach, Norma Ann Jones, Carrie Dhanarajan, David Dhanarajan and Jim Hanback.

             Youth Minister: David Dhanarajan

WHERE TO FIND IT IN THE BIBLE

TURNING THANKS

When

Anxious for dear ones	*Psalms 121; Luke 17*
Business is poor	*Psalms 37, 92; Ecclesiastes 5*
Everything seems going from bad to worse	*2 Timothy 3; Hebrews 13*
Friends seem to go back on you	*Matthew 5; 1 Corinthians 13*
Sorrow overtakes you	*Psalms 46; Matthew 28*
Tempted to do wrong	*Psalms 15, 19, 139; Matthew 4; James 1*
Things look blue	*Psalms 34, 71; Isaiah 40*
You seem too busy	*Ecclesiastes 3:1-15*
You can't go to sleep	*Psalms 4, 56, 130*
You have quarreled	*Matthew 18; Ephesians 4; James 4*
You are weary	*Psalms 95:1-7; Matthew 11*
Worries oppress you	*Psalms 46; Matthew 6*

WHERE TO FIND IT IN THE BIBLE

If You

Are challenged by opposing forces	*Ephesians 6; Philippians 4*
Are facing a crisis	*Job 28:12-28; Proverbs 8, Isaiah 55*
Are jealous	*Psalms 49; James 3*
Are impatient	*Psalms 40, 90; Hebrews 12*
Are bereaved	*1 Corinthians 15; 1 Thessalonians 4:13-5:28 Revelation 21, 22*
Are bored	*2 Kings 5; Job 38; Psalms 103, 104; Ephesians 3*

When

Desiring inward peace	*John 14; Romans 8*
Everything is going well	*Psalms 33:12-22; 100; 1 Timothy 6; James 2:1-17*
Satisfied with yourself	*Proverbs 11; Luke 16*
Seeking the best investment	*Matthew 7*
Starting a new job	*Psalms 1; Proverbs 16; Philippians 3:7-21*

TURNING THANKS

You have been placed in a position of responsibility	*Joshua 1:1-9; Proverbs 2; 2 Corinthians 8:1-15*
Making a new home	*Psalms 127; Proverbs 17; Ephesians 5; Colossians 3; 1 Peter 3:1-17; 1 John 4*
You are out for a good time	*Matthew 15:1-20; 2 Corinthians 3; Galatians 5*
Wanting to live successfully with your fellowmen	*Romans 12*

If You

Bear a grudge	*Luke 6; 2 Corinthians 4; Ephesians 4*
Have experienced severe losses	*Colossians 1; 1 Peter 1*
Have been disobedient	*Isaiah 6; mark 12; Luke 5*
Need forgiveness	*Matthew 23; Luke 15; Philemon*
Are sick or in pain	*Psalms 6, 39, 41, 67; Isaiah 26*

WHERE TO FIND IT IN THE BIBLE

When you

Feel your faith is weak	*Psalms 126, 146; Ephesians 4*
Think God seems far away	*Psalms 25, 125, 138; Luke 10*
Are leaving home	*Psalms 119; Proverbs 3, 4*
Are planning your budget	*Mark 4; Luke 19*
Are becoming lax and indifferent	*Matthew 25; Revelation 3*
Are lonely or fearful	*Psalms 27, 91; Luke 8; 1 Peter 4*
Fear death	*John 11, 16, 20; 2 Corinthians 5; 1 John 3; Revelation 14*
Have sinned	*Psalms 51; Isaiah 53; John 3; 1 John 1*
Want to know the way of prayer	*Kings 8:12-61; Luke 11, 18*
Want a worshipful mood	*Psalms 24, 84, 116; Isaiah 1:10-20; John 4:1-45*
Are concerned with God in national life	*Deuteronomy 8; Psalms 85, 118, 124, Isaiah 41:8-20; Micah 4, 6:6-16*

TURNING THANKS

To Find

The Ten Commandments	*Exodus 20; Deuteronomy 5*
The Shepherd Psalm	*Psalms 23*
The Birth of Jesus	*Matthew 1, 2; Luke 2*
The Beatitudes	*Matthew 5:1-12*
The Lord's Prayer	*Matthew 6:5-15; Luke 11:1-13*
The Sermon on the Mount	*Matthew 5, 6 7*
The Great Commandments	*Matthew 22:34-40*
The Great Commission	*Matthew 28:16-20*
The Parable of the Good Samaritan	*Luke 10*
The Parable of the Prodigal Son	*Luke 15*
The Parable of the Sower	*Matthew 13; Mark 4; Luke 8*
The Last Judgment	*Matthew 25*
The Crucifixion, Death, and Resurrection of Jesus	*Matt. 26, 27, 28; Mark 14, 15, 16; Luke 22, 23, 24; John Chap. 13-21*
The Outpouring of the Holy Spirit	*Acts 2*

NOTES

Mt. Wesley Akin Church of the Nazarene
2013 New Highway 7, Columbia, TN 38401
www.mtwesleyakinnazarene.org

NOTES

NOTES

NOTES

NOTES

www.ingramcontent.com/pod-product-compliance
Lightning Source LLC
Chambersburg PA
CBHW020847090426
42736CB00008B/271